AMAZING
SCIENCE
EXPERIMENTS

AMAZING
SCIENCE
EXPERIMENTS

150 EASY PROJECTS USING EVERYDAY MATERIALS, DEMONSTRATED STEP BY STEP IN 1300 PHOTOGRAPHS!

Consultant CHRIS OXLADE

southwater

CONTENTS

Science at Home 6

Our Restless Earth

Natural Wonders Close to Home

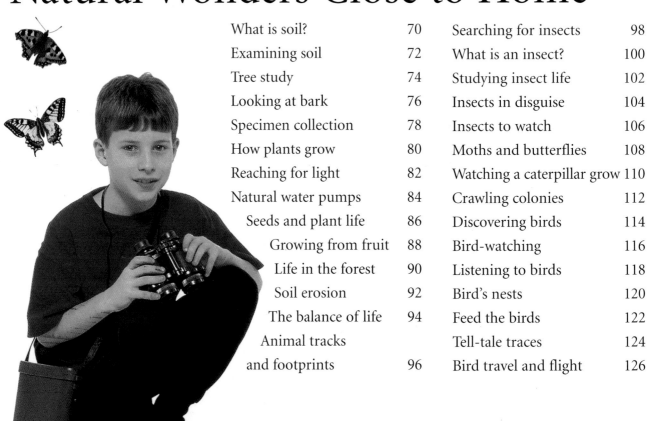

Physical and Material Marvels

Travel and Transport

Science at Home

Science is the search for truth and knowledge. It is the process of finding information about the world around us. It tries to answer questions about how it works. Scientists are people who gather this knowledge of the world. They develop techniques for investigating how things work. They work in controlled environments, such as laboratories, so that they can study the results. We call this experimentation.

Why experiment?

Experiments help you discover and understand how things work and why things happen. When you try ideas out, concepts that seem hard to grasp become easier to understand. This is why scientists experiment—to test their ideas. By experimenting, people invent and perfect machines and processes that make our lives easier. Today, the quality of our lives depends on science for everyday comfort, health and entertainment, transportation and communication.

Innovation and change

This book of experiments demonstrates many of the breakthroughs and discoveries that have had an impact on our lives. The technique of asking questions and trying to answer them through observation and experiment is important to science. The continuous process of discovery and experiment means that scientists come up with different answers. This is why science is always changing. Innovations and inventions change the way we look at the world, so we see it differently. Imagine, for example, what people must have thought the stars were before the telescope was invented to help them see the heavens more clearly.

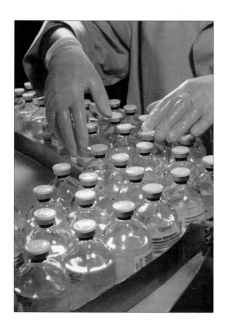

Finding your way around this book

This book is divided into four sections of experiments. Each section explores various specialized areas of science within an everyday theme:

Our Restless Earth looks at the Earth's formation. You will see how weather and geological activities, such as volcanoes and earthquakes, affect the shape of the land.

Natural Wonders Close to Home explores nature and the environment by discovering the habitats in your back-yard or in nearby woods and parks.

Physical and Material Marvels investigates the basic principles of physics and chemistry, from how machines work to construction and building. This section focuses on power and energy, chemical change, light and cameras, electricity and magnets.

Finally, *Travel and Transportation* explores how trains, cars, airplanes, rockets, and ships have developed through history to the present day. This section will also explain how each of these machines work.

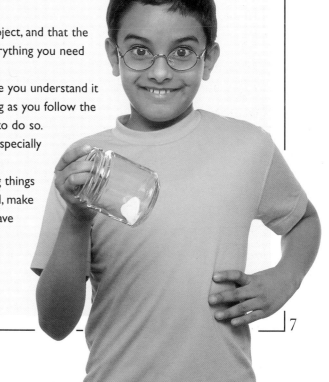

EXPERIMENTING HINTS

• Before you start, tell an adult what you are going to do. Show him or her the experiment and explain where and how you intend to do it.

• Make sure you have all the necessary items required for the project, and that the materials and equipment are clean. You should be able to find everything you need either in your home or from a local store.

• Read the whole project first. Then read each step and make sure you understand it before you begin. All the experiments in this book are safe, as long as you follow the instructions exactly, and ask for adult help when you are advised to do so.

• When you have finished a project, clear everything away safely, especially breakable items, such as glass. Remember to wash your hands!

• Take extra care with experiments that involve electricity, heating things up, and handling chemicals, soil, and glass. If you are using any food, make sure you have permission to use it, and throw it away after you have finished. If a project advises using gloves, be sure to do so.

• Do not worry if an experiment doesn't work, or you miss what happens. Try to work out why it has gone wrong, and do the experiment again. It's all part of the fun!

Our Restless Earth

Earthquakes and volcanoes are a reminder that the Earth's surface is constantly and dramatically changing. Fossils reveal how many kinds of plants and animals that were once alive have now disappeared. Scientists realize that it is part of the Earth's nature to undergo violent changes caused by natural processes that act over billions of years. In the following pages, you can discover how some of these natural processes, such as wind erosion, rivers, and mountain formation, affect the Earth.

Spinning planet

The Earth is like a giant ball spinning in the darkness of Space. The only light falling on it is the light of the Sun, glowing 93 million miles away. The Earth turns once a day, and it orbits the Sun once a year. The experiments on these pages investigate the two ways of moving, and explain why night and day, and the seasons, occur. The ball represents the Earth and the flashlight, the Sun. In the final project, you can make a simple thermometer using water to record changes in temperature from night to day, and from season to season.

North Pole

beams of sunlight

Equator

South Pole

▲ Variable sunlight

The Sun's light does not fall evenly over the Earth, because our planet is round. Imagine three identical beams of sunlight falling on the Earth. One falls on the Equator, and the others on the North and South Poles. The beam falling on the Equator covers a much smaller area, so its energy is more concentrated and the temperature is higher.

YOU WILL NEED

Night and day: felt-tipped pen, plastic ball, piece of thin string, non-hardening modeling material, flashlight.

The seasons: felt-tipped pen, plastic ball, bowl just big enough for the ball to sit on, flashlight, books or a box to set the flashlight on.

Make a thermometer: water, bottle, food coloring, clear straw, reusable adhesive, card, scissors, felt-tipped pen.

Night and day

1 Draw or stick a shape on the ball to represent your country. Stick the string to the ball with modeling material. Tie the string to a rail, such as a towel rail, so that the ball hangs freely.

2 Shine the flashlight on the ball. If the country you live in is on the half of the ball in shadow on the far side, then it is night, because it is facing away from the Sun.

3 Your home country may be on the half of the ball lit by the flashlight instead. If so, it must be daytime here because it is facing the Sun. Keep the torch level, aimed at the middle.

4 Turn the ball from left to right. As you turn the ball, your country will move from the light half to the dark half. You can see how the Sun comes up and goes down as the Earth turns.

The seasons

1 Use the felt-tipped pen to draw a line around the middle of the ball. This represents the Equator. Sit the ball on top of the bowl, so that the Equator line is sloping gently.

2 Put the flashlight on the books so that it shines just above the Equator. It is summer on the half of the ball above the Equator where the flashlight is shining, and winter on the other half of the world.

3 Shine the flashlight on the Equator. It sheds equal light in each half of the ball. This is the equivalent of spring and autumn, when days and nights are a similar length throughout the world.

Solar power ▶

The Sun pours energy on to the Earth as heat and light. The amount of energy received in any one place on the Earth changes with the seasons. This is because the Earth's axis is tilted. In the summer, one half of the Earth tilts toward the Sun, and is warmer. In the winter, it tilts away from the Sun and is colder.

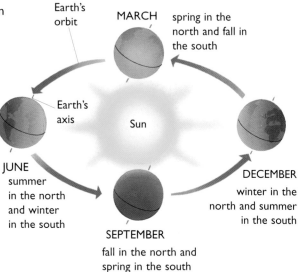

Earth's orbit

MARCH spring in the north and fall in the south

Earth's axis

Sun

JUNE summer in the north and winter in the south

DECEMBER winter in the north and summer in the south

SEPTEMBER fall in the north and spring in the south

Make a thermometer

1 Pour cold water into the bottle until it is about two-thirds full. Add some food coloring. Dip the straw into the water, and seal the neck tightly with reusable adhesive.

4 On a hot day, the Sun's heat will make the air and water expand, forcing the water level in the straw above the room temperature mark. Cool the thermometer in the fridge. Mark the different levels.

2 Blow down the straw to force some extra air into the bottle. After a few seconds, the extra air pressure inside will force the water level to rise up the straw.

3 Cut the card and slot it in over the straw. Let the bottle stand for a while. Make a mark on the card by the water level to show room temperature. Take your thermometer outside.

Phases of the Moon

The Moon is Earth's closest neighbor in space. We know more about the Moon than about any other heavenly body because astronauts have landed on it and explored the surface. The Moon is Earth's only satellite. It measures 2,160 miles across, about a quarter of the size of the Earth. It circles the Earth at a distance of about 239,000 miles, and makes the journey about once a month. The Moon does not give out any light of its own. We see it because it reflects light from the Sun. The sunlight illuminates different parts of the Moon as the month goes by. This makes the Moon seem to change shape. The Moon spins around slowly as it circles the Earth, so the same side is always turned toward the Earth.

We only see the Moon lit up completely once a month, but you do not have to wait a month to see the changes in its shape or phases. The project here will show you in just a few minutes how the Moon goes through its phases!

▲ Face of the Moon

This picture shows a view of the Moon from the Earth. When the whole of the Moon is lit up like this, we call it a full Moon. The darker regions on the surface are great, dusty plains called seas, or maria. The lighter areas are highlands. These are pitted with craters that are sometimes hundreds of miles across. Mountains on the Moon rise to more than 18,000 feet.

Make your own Moon

YOU WILL NEED
soccer or beach ball, glue, glue brush, glass, tinfoil, scissors, reusable adhesive, flashlight.

1 Make sure that you have washed and dried your ball thoroughly before using! Paint glue all over the ball. Rest it on a glass or something similar, to keep it still.

2 Carefully cut the tinfoil into large square sheets. Wrap up the ball in the tinfoil. Try to make sure that the wrapping is as smooth as possible. You now have your Moon!

3 Place your Moon on a table. Wedge a small ball of reusable adhesive under the ball. This will hold it firm and stop it from rolling off the table.

4 Get your friend to stand at one side of the table to shine a flashlight with a strong beam on your Moon. Go to the opposite side of the table. Look at your Moon with the main lights out.

5 Gradually move around the table, still looking at your Moon, which is lit up one side by the flashlight. You will see the different shapes it takes. These shapes are the Moon's phases.

Going through the phases ▸

When you are opposite your friend in the project, the side of the ball facing you is dark. This is what happens once a month in the night sky. We can only see a thin sliver of light, which we call a new or crescent Moon. As you move around the table, more of the ball is lit by the flashlight. All of it will be lit when you are behind your friend. When this happens to the real Moon, we describe it as full. As you continue moving around, the ball gradually fades into darkness. When you are opposite your friend again, you will see a new Moon again.

crescent Moon

first quarter phase

full Moon

last quarter phase

crescent Moon

The rise and fall of tides

▲ Close neighbor

The Moon is a lifeless desert of rock. It has no atmosphere to protect it from the Sun's dangerous rays, and no water to sustain life. The shape of the Moon appears to change during the month. We call these changes in shape the Moon's phases. It takes the Moon 29½ days to change from a slim crescent to a full circle and back again.

The Earth appears blue from the darkness of Space. This is because more than 70 percent of its surface is covered with oceans. The seas make up more than one million million million tons of seawater.

Every 12 hours or so, the seawater rises, then falls back again. These rises and falls are called the tides. When the water is rising, we say the tide is flowing. When it is falling, we say the tide is ebbing. The movement of the ocean waters is caused by the Moon and by the Earth spinning. Gravity pulls the Moon and Earth together. As the Earth turns, the Moon pulls at the ocean water directly beneath it, causing the water to rise. A similar rise in sea level occurs on the opposite side of the Earth, where the water bulges out as a result of the Earth spinning. At these places, there is a high tide. Some six hours later, the Earth has turned 90°. The sea then falls to its lowest point and there is a low tide.

The two experiments opposite explain how the oceans rise and fall without any change in the amount of seawater, and how the tidal bulges of water stay in the same place below the Moon, as the Earth spins beneath it.

How tides occur

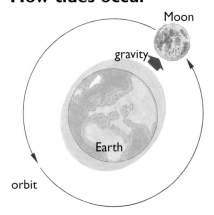

Tides rise beneath the Moon as the Earth turns. The gravity of the Moon tugs at the oceans, pulling the water around with it.

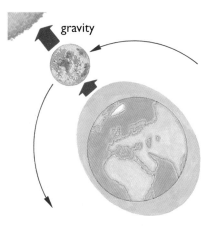

Once every two weeks, the Sun and the Moon line up with the Earth. Their combined pull creates a spring tide, where the tides are higher than usual.

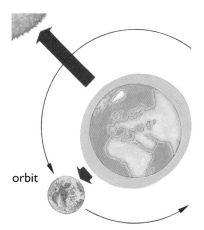

One week later, the Sun and the Moon are at right angles to each other. Pulling in different directions, they create a lower tide than usual, called a neap tide.

High and low tide

1 Place the bowl on a firm, flat surface, then half fill it with water. Place the ball gently in the water so that it floats in the middle of the bowl, as shown in the picture.

2 Place both hands on top of the ball, and push it down into the water gently but firmly. Look what happens to the level of the water. It rises in a "high tide".

3 Let the ball gently rise again. Now you can see the water in the bowl dropping again. So the tide has risen and fallen, even though the amount of water is unchanged.

The tidal bulge

YOU WILL NEED

High and low tide: plastic bowl, water, plastic ball to represent the world.

The tidal bulge: strong glue, one 8in length and two 16in lengths of thin string, plastic ball to represent the world, plastic bowl, hand drill, water.

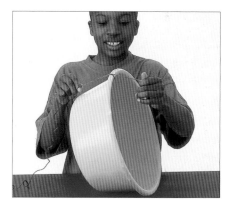

1 Glue the 8in length of the string very firmly to the ball and leave it to dry. Meanwhile, ask an adult to drill two holes in the rim of the bowl, one on each side.

2 Thread a 16in length of string through each hole, and knot the string around the rim. Half fill the plastic bowl with water and float the ball in the water.

3 Ask a friend to pull the string on the ball toward him or her. There is now more water on one side of the ball than the other. This is called a tidal bulge.

4 The Moon pulls on the water as well as the Earth. So now ask the friend to hold the ball in place, while both of you pull out the strings attached to the bowl until it distorts.

5 There is now a tidal bulge on each side of the world. One of you slowly turn the ball. Now you can see how, in effect, the tidal bulges move around the world as the world turns.

Ocean waves and currents

▲ **Powerful seas**

In stormy weather, giant waves rear up and crash down, turning the sea into a raging turmoil.

The sea is rarely still. Even on a calm day, you will see ripples on the surface. Waves move over the ocean's surface. They are driven mainly by the wind. The stronger the winds, and the longer the fetch (the distance they have traveled), the bigger and higher the waves are. Waves usually only affect the surface of the water. As they travel, the water itself does not move. It just moves up and down as the wave passes through it. At a very deep level in some oceans, the water does move in giant streams called ocean currents. These can be hot or cold, and can affect the world's climate. Ocean currents are usually caused by differences in the water's saltiness or temperature, rather than by the wind.

The first project shows how waves are made, and the second, how currents are set up by the wind blowing. Currents such as the ones in the third project happen on a much larger scale in the world's major oceans.

wave approaches float

float maintains position

wave travels, float does not

▲ **Wave goodbye**

The diagrams above show how waves travel across the water surface, while objects floating on the water hardly move at all.

Making waves

YOU WILL NEED
rectangular plastic pitcher, jug, water, bathtub or inflatable pool, non-hardening modeling material.

1 Place the bowl on the floor or on a table. Choose a place where it does not matter if a little water spills over. Fill the bowl with water until it almost reaches the brim.

2 Blow very gently over the surface of the water. You will see that the water begins to ripple where you blow on it. This is how ocean waves are formed by air movement.

3 Fill the bathtub or pool with water. Blow gently along the length of the bath or pool. Blow at the same strength as in step 2, and from the same height above the water.

4 Keep blowing for a minute or so. Notice that the waves are bigger in the bathtub or pool, even though you are not blowing harder. This is because they reach farther across the water.

5 Now drop a small piece of modeling material into the water. Watch how it sets up waves. Ripples travel out in circles from where the modeling material entered the water.

Ocean currents

YOU WILL NEED

rectangular plastic bowl, pitcher, water, talcum powder.

1 Place the bowl on the floor or on a table. Choose a place where it does not matter if a little water spills over. Fill the bowl with water until it almost reaches the rim.

2 Scatter a small amount of talcum powder over the water. Use just enough powder to make a very fine film over the water's surface. The less you use, the better.

3 Blow very gently across the water from the center of one side of the bowl to the other. You will see how the water starts to move. Ocean currents begin to move in the same way.

4 Keep blowing, and the powder swirls in two circles as it hits the far side. This is what happens when currents hit continents. One current turns clockwise, the other turns anticlockwise.

Changing coastlines

Of all the natural forces that erode (wear away) the land, the sea is the most powerful. It carries sand particles that act like a grindstone on the shore. Waves are forced into cracks in the rocks. They widen the cracks, eventually breaking up the rock face. Huge cliffs are carved out of mountains, broad platforms are sliced back through rocks, and houses are left dangling over the edges of the land.

New land can also be created at the ocean's edge. Where headland cliffs are being eroded by waves, the bays between may fill with sand. On coasts where the sea is shallow, waves build beaches of shingle, sand, and mud. The first experiment demonstrates the destructive effect of the sea when it hits the shore. The second project shows how waves make ripples on sandy beaches.

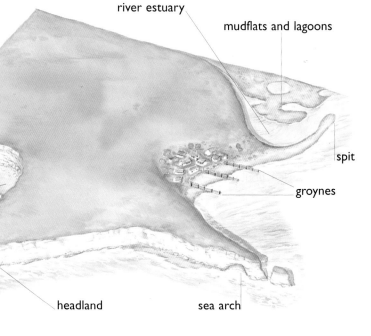

river estuary

mudflats and lagoons

spit

groynes

bayhead beach

stump

sea stack

headland

sea arch

▲ Everchanging landscape
The sea's power to build and destroy a coastline can be seen in this picture. Coastal areas that are exposed to the full force of the waves are eroded into steep cliffs. Headlands are worn back, leaving behind stacks, stumps, and arches. In more sheltered places, the sand piles up to form beaches, or waves may carry material along the coast to build spits and mudflats.

▲ Relentless assault
The sea is at its most spectacular at the edges of big oceans, where the waves are big and powerful. In time, their continuous assault on the land will break up the toughest rocks into tiny pieces.

Attacking the shore

1 Mix a little water with the sand in a bucket, until it is very wet and sticks firmly together. Then pack the sand into a wedge shape at one end of the tank.

2 Carefully pour water into the empty end of the tank, so as not to disturb the sand too much. Fill the tank until the water level comes about two-thirds of the way up the sloping sand.

3 Make gentle waves in the water on the opposite side of the sand. Notice how the waves gradually wear away the sloping sand. This is what happens on a sandy seashore.

How ripples are formed in sand

YOU WILL NEED

Making waves: sand, plastic bucket, water tank, water, pitcher.

How ripples are formed in sand: heavy filled round can, round dishwashing bowl, pitcher, water, fine, clean sand, spoon.

1 Place a heavy can in the centre of the dishwashing bowl, then fill the bowl with water to at least half way. The water should not cover more than two-thirds of the can.

2 Sprinkle a little sand into the bowl to create a thin layer about ¼in deep. Spread the sand until it is even, then let it settle into a flat layer at the bottom of the bowl.

3 Stir the water gently with the spoon. Drag the spoon in a circle around can tin. As the water begins to swirl, stir faster with the spoon, but keep the movement smooth.

4 As you stir faster, lift the spoon out and let the water swirl around by itself. The sand will start to develop ripples. As you stir faster, the ripples become more defined.

Water on the move

Rivers start high in the hills and wind their way down toward the sea, or sometimes, a lake. At its start, a river is a tiny stream tumbling down the slopes. It is formed by rain running off a mountainside, or by water bubbling up from a spring. As the water flows downhill, it is joined by other streams and grows bigger.

The first project shows how water shapes the landscape by physically eroding (wearing away) the rock. The second experiment demonstrates how in some places, erosion can be a chemical process, in which water dissolves the rock and carries it away.

Over millions of years, a river can carve a gorge deep through solid rock, or deposit (lay down) a vast plain of fine mud called silt. The great rivers of the world take millions of tons of mud, rock, and sand from the land every day and carry them into the sea. If the river meets a low-lying shoreline, the sediment is dropped. It may spread out into a fan-shaped muddy plain called a delta. When this happens, the river is forced to branch out into smaller streams as it flows into the sea. You can see how this happens in the third experiment.

upper reaches

middle reaches

lower reaches

◄ The course of a river

As it moves across the land, a river changes in character. In the upper reaches, it is a fast-flowing, tumbling stream that cuts down through steep, narrow valleys. Lower down, it broadens and deepens into a river. Eventually, it moves across a broad floodplain before reaching the sea.

The destructive power of water

1 Put one end of a baking sheet on a brick. Put the other end of the baking sheet on a lower tray or bowl, so that it slopes downward. Make a sandcastle on the baking tray.

2 Slowly drip water over the sandcastle. Watch the sand crumble and form a new shape. This happens because the sand erodes away where the water hits it.

3 Make sure that the water flows down the center of the baking sheet. This way, the water hits the middle of the sand castle, eroding the center to form a natural stack.

Chemical erosion

1 Build a pile of brown sugar on a baking sheet. Imagine that it is a mountain made of a soluble rock (that dissolves in water). Press the sugar down firmly, and shape it to a point.

2 Drip water on your sugar mountain. It will erode as the water dissolves the sugar. The water running off should be brown, because it contains dissolved brown sugar.

Making a delta

1 Use scissors to trim the top of the cardboard container so that it is about 4-6in deep. Now take the two plastic garbage bags to make the box waterproof.

2 Cover the inside of the box with the garbage bags and tape them securely at each end of the box. Make sure that the seal between the garbage bags is secure.

3 Using the trowel, carefully spread a layer of sand over the bottom of the sheet until the sand is about 1½-2in deep. Flatten the sand with the trowel until it is smooth.

4 Rest one end of the container on a woodblock or something similar, to make a slope. Pour water from the jug onto the sand in the middle of the higher end.

5 If you continue pouring, you will find that the water gradually washes away a gully through the sand. It deposits sand it has washed away at the lower end in a delta region.

Cloud and rain

Water moves around the Earth and its atmosphere in a continuous process called the water cycle. Heat from the Sun causes water from oceans, lakes, and rivers to evaporate into water vapor. Water is also released into the atmosphere from plants in a process called transpiration Flowers and trees take up water from their roots. They use some and release the rest back out through their leaves - water vapor rises into the atmosphere. It cools as it rises, and changes back into tiny droplets of liquid water. This is called condensation. The droplets gather together and form clouds. When the water in the atmosphere becomes too heavy to be held in the air, it returns to the Earth's surface as precipitation (dew, rain, sleet, and snow). The land has a fresh supply of water, and so the water cycle continues.

The first experiment shows you how water changes to vapor and back again, when a cold surface makes the water vapor condense into water droplets. In the second project, you can make a simple rain gauge to measure the amount of rain you get where you live. If you live in a desert region, you may have to wait a long time!

cloud of ice crystals

cloud of water droplets

water vapour rises

▲ Forming clouds

Clouds form when warm air containing water vapor rises into the air and cools. The vapor turns into droplets of water, forming clouds. If the air is very cold, the vapor turns into a cloud of tiny ice crystals.

YOU WILL NEED
heat-proof pitcher, water, pan, oven mitts, plate.

Water vapor

I Fill up the pitcher with water from the hot water tap. Pour the water into the pan. Switch on one of the rings on the stove and place the pan on it.

2 Heat the water until it is boiling and steam is rising. Lift the plate with the oven gloves. Hold it upside down above the saucepan. After a few minutes, turn off the heat.

3 Take the plate away, using the oven mitts. You will see that the plate is covered with drops of water. This is water vapor that has cooled and turned back into liquid.

Make a weather vane

I Stick a ball of reusable adhesive to the middle of the lid of the pot. Ask an adult to pierce a hole in the bottom of the pot with the scissors. Place the pot on top of the lid.

2 Slide the stick into one of the straws. Trim the end of the stick so that it is a little shorter than the straw. Push the straw and stick through the hole in the pot and into the adhesive.

3 Cut out a square of card. Mark each corner with a point of the compass—N, E, S, W. Fold in half and snip a hole in the middle. Carefully slip the card over the straw.

4 Cut out two card triangles. Stick them to each end of the second straw to form an arrow head and tail. Put a ball of reusable adhesive in the top of the first straw in the pot.

5 Push a pin through the middle of the arrow. Stick the pin into the reusable adhesive in the first straw. Be careful not to prick your finger when you handle the pin.

6 Attach your weather vane to a plywood base using a piece of reusable adhesive. Test it for use— the arrow should spin around freely when you blow on it.

7 Take your weather vane outside and use a compass to point it in the right direction. You can now discover the direction the wind is blowing.

Turning the sails ▶

The miniature windmills on this toy spin faster the harder you blow on them. The sails of real windmills also spin faster as the speed of the wind increases. As a result, windmills need a 'governor'. This device regulates the speed of the sails' rotation, so they are not damaged in very windy weather.

Recording weather

Meteorologists gather information about the weather from satellites, balloons, and other instruments. Powerful computers help them to analyze the data. Using this information, meteorologists draw weather maps. These can show the state of the weather at any one time, or they can be a forecast of weather in the future. The maps use symbols to represent conditions such as rainfall and wind direction.

You can set up your own weather station to record daily conditions with a few simple devices. You will be able to use some of the instruments you have made in other projects, such as the weather vane, hygrometer, and rain gauge. You will also need to buy a thermometer to measure the temperature. Take measurements with your weather instruments every day. Write them down in a special weather book. Also, make a note of what the weather is like in general—fine, cloudy, drizzly, frosty, and so on. Don't forget to make a note of the date!

Meteorologists look at records from the past to discover changes in climate. The project opposite shows you how to make your own discoveries about climate changes, by looking at the record of tree growth.

▲ Forecasting rain

A hygrometer will gauge the amount of moisture in the air. When the pointer tilts up on the scale, the air is moist and rain may be on the way.

▲ Measuring rainfall

A rain gauge will tell you how much rain has fallen. Rainfall is collected over a set period in a jar or measuring bottle, and the amount is recorded.

▲ Wind direction

A windmill shows how hard the wind is blowing. A weather vane will tell you the wind's direction. The arrow points in the direction that the wind is blowing from. So if the arrow points west, the wind is a west wind.

The wooden weather record

YOU WILL NEED

newly cut log, decorating paintbrush, ruler with ¹⁄₁₆in measurements, metric graph paper, pen or pencil.

1 Ask a tree surgeon, the local council, or a sawmill for a newly cut slice of log. Use the paintbrush to brush away the dust and dirt from the slice of wood.

2 When the log slice is clean, examine it closely. Look at the pattern of rings. They are small in the middle, and get bigger and bigger toward the outer edge of the log.

3 Each ring is a year's growth. So count the rings out from the middle carefully. This tells you how old the tree is. If there are 105 rings, for instance, the tree is 105 years old.

4 Using a ruler, measure the width of each ring. Start from the center and work outward. Ask a friend to write down the widths as you call them out.

5 On graph paper, mark five squares for each year along the bottom. Mark widths for the rings up the side, five squares for each ¹⁄₁₆in. Plot your measurements as dots for each year.

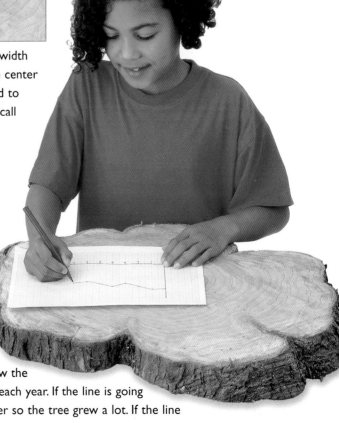

6 Join the dots with a line. This line shows how the weather has changed with each year. If the line is going up, the weather was warmer so the tree grew a lot. If the line falls, the weather was colder so the tree grew less.

Broken Earth

The surface of the Earth is not one piece but cracked, like a broken eggshell, into giant slabs. There are about 20 of these huge pieces of rock which are called tectonic plates. Tectonic plates are not held in one place, but slide around the Earth. They move very slowly—at about the pace of a fingernail growing. But tectonic plates are so gigantic that their movement has dramatic effects on the Earth's surface. Earthquakes and volcanoes happen where plates slide apart or past each other, or collide. Colliding plates also push up mountain ranges.

The continents drift around the world on tectonic plates. Once, they were all joined together in one huge continent called Pangaea. Around 200 million years ago, the tectonic plates beneath Pangaea began to move apart, carrying fragments of the continent with them. These fragments slowly drifted into the positions they are in now. The experiment opposite demonstrates how the continents may have once been, and how they move.

▲ Patterns of earthquakes

The Earth's rigid shell is called the lithosphere, from the Greek word lithos (stone). It is broken into the huge fragments shown on this map. The African plate is gigantic, underlying not only Africa, but half of the Atlantic Ocean too. The Cocos plate under the West Indies is much smaller. Black dots mark the origins of major earthquakes over a year. See how they coincide with the plate margins.

▲ Pulling apart

Right down the middle of the sea bed in the Atlantic Ocean, there is a giant crack where the tectonic plates are pulling apart. Molten (melted) rock from the Earth's interior wells up into the crack. As it cools, it solidifies (becomes solid) to form the mid-ocean ridge.

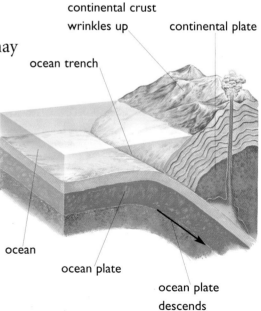

▲ Pushing together

In many places, tectonic plates slowly crunch together with enormous force. As they collide, one plate may be forced under the other. Earthquakes and volcanoes are often the result.

A continental jigsaw

1 Find the continents of North and South America, Europe, and Africa in an atlas. Trace the outlines of the shape of these continents onto tracing paper.

2 Stick the tracing paper on to different colored sheets of card. Then carefully cut around the outlines of the continents you have drawn from the atlas.

3 Move the eastern (right-hand) coasts of North and South America up to the western (left-hand) coasts of Europe and Africa to see how well they fit together.

4 You will find that the coastlines of the Americas, Europe, and Africa fit together very well. Scientists believe that these continents were once joined together in this way.

5 The continents of the Americas, Europe, and Africa sit on plates that are moving in opposite directions. Use the continent cards you have made in the above project to see how they drift apart. Fold a large sheet of card in half, and attach paper clips along the fold. Drape it over two boxes. Stick the Americas on one sheet, and Europe and Africa on the other. Push upward on the fold, and see the continents move apart.

Restless Earth

The movement of rocks that causes earthquakes usually occurs deep inside the Earth's crust. The exact point at which the rocks start to break or fracture is known as the focus. This can lie as deep as hundreds of miles or as close as tens of miles down. The most violent disturbance on the surface occurs at a point directly above the focus, called the epicenter. The closer the focus is, the more destructive the earthquake. San Francisco, in California, sits near a line of weakness in the Earth's crust known as the San Andreas Fault. The fault marks the boundary of the eastern Pacific plate and the North American plate. As they try to slide past each other, they make the ground shake violently. Earthquakes and volcanoes occur around the boundaries of all the plates on the Earth's surface.

epicentre

cracked rocks

fault line

focus

▲ **Earthquake alert**

Most earthquakes originate in rock many miles below the surface, at the focus. The most intense vibrations on the surface are felt immediately above the focus, at the epicenter.

YOU WILL NEED

Tremors: set of dominoes, card.

Quakes: scissors, strong rubber band, ruler, plastic seed tray (without holes), piece of card, salt.

Tremors

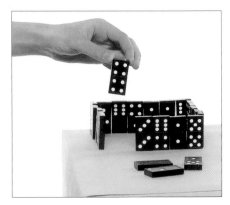

I This project investigates how energy in earthquake waves (tremors) varies with distance. Near the end of a table, build a simple house out of dominoes. Stand them up on their edges.

2 Place the card on the dominoes to make the roof of your house. Many people in earthquake zones live in the simplest of houses, built not too differently from this one.

3 Go to the opposite end of the table and hit it with your hand, but not too hard. Your domino house probably shakes, but still stays standing. Now hit the table at the other end.

4 The waves you create when you hit the table are strong enough to knock down the house. When you hit the other end of the table, the waves are too weak to knock it down.

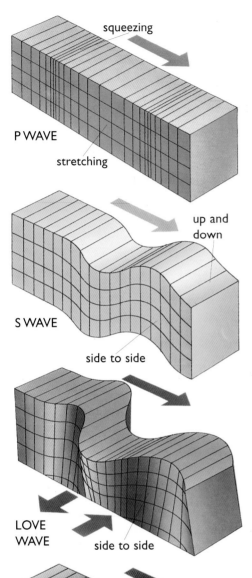

P WAVE

squeezing

stretching

S WAVE

up and down

side to side

LOVE WAVE

side to side

RAYLEIGH WAVE

rippling up and down

▲ How earthquakes move

The enormous energy released by an earthquake travels through the ground in the form of waves. The P (primary) wave compresses, then stretches rocks it passes through. The S (secondary) wave produces a side-to-side and up-and-down action. Love waves travel on the surface, making the ground move from side to side. Rayleigh waves are surface waves that move up and down.

Quakes

1 With the scissors, cut the rubber band at one end to make a long strip. This represents a layer of rock inside the Earth before it is affected by an earthquake.

2 Measure the rubber strip with a ruler. This represents the original length of the rock in the ground. Make a note of how long the rubber is at this stage.

3 Stretch the rubber band and hold it tightly above the tray. In the same way, rocks get stretched by pulling forces inside the Earth during an earthquake.

4 Ask a friend to hold the card on top of the rubber strip and sprinkle some salt on it. The salt layer on the card represents the surface of the ground above the stretched rock layer.

5 Now let go of the ends of the rubber strip. Notice how the salt grains on the card are thrown around. This was caused by the energy released when the rubber shrank.

6 Finally, measure the rubber strip again. You will find that it is slightly longer than it was at the start. Rocks are often permanently stretched a little after an earthquake.

Measuring earthquakes

Scientists who study earthquakes are called seismologists. They have a variety of instruments to gather data. The Newton's cradle experiment below explains how waves (tremors) work. The other projects show two ways in which seismologists detect how the ground moves at the beginning of an earthquake. A gravimeter measures small changes in gravity. The tiltmeter detects whether rock layers are tilting.

YOU WILL NEED
Newton's cradle: large beads, wool, tape, cane, four wooden blocks.
Gravimeter: masking tape, ruler, pen, large jar, non hardening modeling material, rubber band, toothpick, pencil.

Newton's cradle

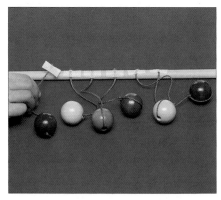

1 Tie the beads to the ends of the wool threads. Tape the other ends to the cane. Make sure the threads are all the same length, and that the beads just touch when they hang down.

2 Prop up the cane at both ends on a pair of woodblocks supported by more blocks underneath. Secure the ends of the cane with tape. Lift up the bead at one end of the row and let go.

3 The bead at the other end flies up. The energy of the falling bead at one end travels as a pressure wave through the middle ones. It reaches the bead at the other end and pushes it away.

Gravimeter

1 Draw a scale on a strip of masking tape using a ruler and pen. Stick the scale on the jar. On a real instrument, this would measure slight changes in gravity.

2 Bury one end of a rubber band in a ball of modeling material. Stick a toothpick in at right angles to the band, to act as a pointer. Pass the pencil through the loop of the band.

3 Lower the ball into the jar, so that the pointer tip is close to the scale. Attach the pencil on top with modelling material. Move the jar up or down, and the pointer moves down or up the scale.

Tiltmeter

YOU WILL NEED

hole punch, two transparent plastic cups, transparent plastic tubing, nonhardening modeling material, pen, masking tape, ruler, wooden board, adhesive, food coloring, pitcher of water.

1 Use the hole punch to make a hole in the side of each plastic cup, just about halfway down. Be careful not to prick your fingers. Ask an adult to help you if you prefer.

2 Push one end of the tubing into the hole in one of the cups. Seal it tight with modeling material. Put the other end in the hole in the other cup, and seal it as well.

3 Using the pen, draw identical scales on two strips of the masking tape. Use a ruler and mark regular spaces. Stick the scales at the same height on the side of the cups.

4 Stick the cups to the wooden baseboard with adhesive. Arrange them so that the tube between is pulled straight, but make sure it doesn't pull out.

6 Your tiltmeter is now ready for use. When it is level, the water levels in the cups are the same. When it tilts, the water levels change as water runs through the tube from one cup to the other. Scientists use tiltometers to detect whether rock layers are moving by comparing the water levels in two connected containers.

5 Add food coloring to water in the pitcher, and pour it into each of the cups. Make sure to fill the cups, so that the water level reaches over the openings to the tubes.

Do-it-yourself seismograph

There are hundreds of seismic (from the Greek word *seismos*, meaning earthquake) centers around the world. Within minutes of a quake, scientists begin analyzing data from their seismographs. They then compare notes with scientists in other countries. The Italian scientist, Luigi Palmieri, built the first seismograph in 1856. All seismographs work on the same principle. They have a light frame attached to the ground, and a heavy weight attached to the frame by a spring. The heavy weight has a high inertia, which means it is more difficult to set in motion than a light object. When an earthquake happens, the frame shakes with the ground, but the heavy weight stays in the same place because of inertia. The movement of the frame around the steady weight is recorded by a pen on a roll of paper, which draws a wavy line. The same principle of the inertia of a heavy weight is used to detect tremors in the seismograph shown here.

▲ Catching the tremors

The Chinese invented a type of seismograph in A.D. 132. When there was an earthquake, a ball was released from one of the dragons and fell into a frog's mouth. This showed the direction of the vibrations. The instrument detected a earth tremor 300km away.

Building a seismograph

YOU WILL NEED

cardboard box, bradawl, tape,

nonhardening modeling material,

pencil, felt-tipped pen, string,

piece of card.

1 The cardboard box will become the frame of your seismograph. It needs to be made of very stiff card. The open part of the box will be the front of your instrument.

2 Make a hole in what will be the top of the frame with the bradawl. If the box feels flimsy, strengthen it by taping around the corners, as shown in the picture.

3 Roll a piece of modeling material into a ball, and make a hole in it with the pencil. Push the felt-tipped pen through the modeling material to reach a little way beyond the hole.

4 This will be the pointer of your seismograph and make a record of earthquake vibrations. Tie one end of the piece of string to the top of the pen.

5 Thread the other end of the string through the hole in the top of the box. Now stand the box upright and pull the string through until the pen hangs free.

6 Tie the top end of the string to the pencil, and roll the pencil to take up the slack. When the pen is at the right height (just touching the bottom), tape the pencil into place.

7 Place the card in the bottom of the box underneath the pen. If you have adjusted it properly, the tip of the pen should just touch the card to mark it.

8 Your seismograph is now ready to use. It uses the same principle as a proper seismograph. The heavy bob, or pendulum, will be less affected by shaking motions than the frame.

9 You do not have to wait for an earthquake to test your seismograph. Just shake or tilt the frame. The suspended pen does not move, but it marks the piece of card, giving you your very own seismograph.

Slips and faults

Every earthquake, from the slightest tremor to the violent shaking that destroys buildings, has the same basic cause. Two plates of rock grind past each other along a fault line where the Earth's crust has fractured. Friction between the plates means they do not slide past each other smoothly, but jam and then jump. The first experiment on the opposite page shows how friction at fault lines causes great destructive energy.

direction of movement

fault plane

Crustal plates float on top of the mantle beneath. The oceanic crust is heavier and denser than the continental crust so it sits lower down. The experiment below demonstrates this.

There are several kinds of fault. When blocks slide past each other horizontally, it is called a transform, or strike-slip fault. In a normal fault, the rocks are pulling apart, and one block slides down the other. In a thrust fault, the blocks are pressing together, causing one to ride up above the other. The second project on the opposite page shows how these movements create landforms, such as mountains and valleys.

▲ Making mountains

Fault mountains form by the slow, unstoppable movement of tectonic plates. This puts rocks under such huge stress that they sometimes crack. Such cracks are called faults. Where they occur, huge blocks of rock slip up and down past each other, creating cliffs. In places, a whole series of giant blocks may be thrown up together, creating a new mountain range. The Black Mountains in Germany are an example of block mountains formed in this way.

Floating plates

YOU WILL NEED
woodblock, polystyrene block, bowl of water

1 The two blocks should be roughly the same size and shape. Polystyrene represents the continental crust, wood the oceanic crust, and water the fluid mantle.

2 Place the blocks in the water. The polystyrene floats higher, because it is less dense, just as the continental crust floats higher on the mantle. Which of the two blocks weighs more?

Fault movements

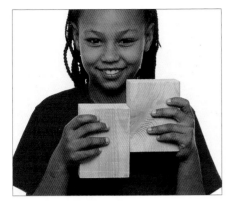

1 Hold a block in each hand so that the sides of the blocks are touching. Pushing gently, try to make the blocks slide past each other. You will find this easy.

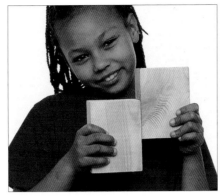

2 Wet the sides of the blocks with the oil, and try to slide them again. You should find that it is easier, because the oil has lessened the friction between the blocks.

3 Pin sheets of sandpaper on the sides of the blocks, and try to make them slide now. You will find it much harder. The sandpaper is rough, and increases friction between the blocks.

Building mountains

> ### YOU WILL NEED
>
> **Fault movements:** two woodblocks, baby oil, thumb tacks, sheets of sandpaper.
>
> **Building mountains:** 8in square sheet of paper, nonhardening modeling material in various colors, rolling pin, modeling tool.

1 On the sheet of paper, roll out several flat sheets of modeling material, each one a different color. The sheets should be about the same size as the sheet of paper.

2 Place the square, flat sheets of modeling material on top of each other to make a layered block. The different colored layers are like the layers of rock strata in the Earth's crust.

3 Lay the layered block flat on the table. With a modeling tool, carefully make two cuts in the clay—one toward the left, and the other toward the right, as shown above.

4 Make two small balls. Lift each of the outside pieces that you have cut onto a ball, as shown above. This forms a block mountain separated by a rift valley.

block mountains

rift valley

The crust breaks away at a rift zone where the plates are moving apart. Uplifted rock strata form block mountains, and a descending mass of rock creates the valley.

Building fold mountains

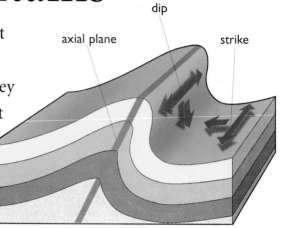

Most high mountains are a part of great ranges that stretch for hundreds of miles. They may look as though they have been there forever, but geologically they are very young. They have all been thrown up in the last few hundred million years.

The biggest—and youngest—mountain ranges in the world, such as the Himalayas and the Andes, are fold mountains. They started life as flat layers of rock called strata. Layers of rock are laid down over millennia. Some strata form as successive layers of sediments, such as sand, mud, and seashells, settle on the ocean floor. Other strata may be made up of molten rock thrown up from the heart of the Earth by volcanoes.

Fold mountains are layers of rock that have been crunched up by pressure—in a similar way to the pressure you will be exerting in these two projects. In real mountain formation, two of the tectonic plates that make up the Earth's surface push against each other, forcing the rock layers along their edges into massive folds. As the layers of rock are squeezed, the folds become more exaggerated.

▲ Anatomy of a fold
Geologists describe an upfold as an anticline, and a downfold as a syncline. The dip is the direction the fold is sloping. The angle of dip is how steep the slope is. The strike is the line along the fold. The axial plane is an imaginary line through the center of the fold—this may be vertical, horizontal, or at any angle in between.

YOU WILL NEED
thin rug

Simple folds

1 Find an uncarpeted floor, and lay the rug down with one short, straight edge up against a wall. Make sure the long edge of the rug is at a right angle to the wall.

2 Now push the outer edge of the rug toward the wall. See how the rug crumples. This is how rock layers buckle to form mountains, as tectonic plates push against each other.

3 Push the rug up against the wall even more, and you will see some of the folds turn right on top of each other. These are like folded-over strata or layers, called nappes.

Complex folds

I Roll out the modeling material into flat sheets in different colours, each about ¼in thick. Cut into strips about the same width as the woodblocks. Square off the ends.

2 Lay the strips carefully on top of each other, in alternating colors or in a series of colors. These strips represent the layers or strata of rock.

3 Place the woodblocks at either end of the strips. Lay the bars of wood down on either side of the strips to prevent them from twisting sideways.

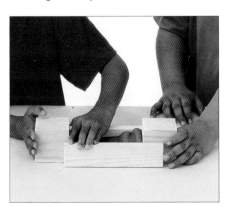

4 Ask a friend to hold onto one block, while you push the other toward it. As you push, the effect is similar to two tectonic plates slowly pushing together.

5 From time to time, stop and pull the bars of away wood, so that you can have a look at what is happening. As you push harder, see how the layers crumple increasingly and start to turn over themselves. Overlapping folds like this are called nappes.

Fire down below

Volcanoes begin many miles beneath the Earth's surface. The landscape that makes up the surface of our planet is only a thin "crust" of hard rock compared with what lies beneath. First, there is a thick layer of semiliquid rock called the mantle. Then comes an intensely hot core of iron and nickel. This reaches temperatures of $6,700^{oF}$, but the surrounding pressure is so great it cannot melt.

Heat moves out from the core to the mantle. Here, rocks are semiliquid and move like molasses. They cannot melt completely because of pressure.

In some parts of the upper mantle, though, rocks do melt and are called magma. This collects in chambers, and it may bubble up through gaps in the crust via a volcano. You can watch how solids such as magma react to heat—become soft, then melt, and finally flow—in this project.

Most of the world's volcanoes lie along fault lines, where plates (sections of the Earth's crust) meet. A few, however, such as those in Hawaii, lie over hot spots beneath the Earth's crust. A hot spot is an area on a plate where hot rock from the mantle bubbles up underneath. The plate above moves, but the hot spot stays in the same place in the mantle. The hot spot keeps burning through the plate to make a volcano in a new place. A string of inactive (dead) volcanoes is left behind, as the plate moves over the hot spot. Some form islands above the ocean surface. Others, called sea mounts, remain submerged.

mantle

outer core

inner core

crust

continent

ocean

▲ Inside the Earth

Our planet is made up of different layers. The top layer is the hard crust. It is thinnest under the oceans, where it is only about 3-6 miles thick. Underneath the crust is a thick layer of semiliquid rock called the mantle. Beneath the mantle is a layer of liquid metal, mainly iron and nickel, that makes up the Earth's outer core. The inner core at the center is solid, and is made up of iron and other metals.

chains of dead volcanoes

active volcano

ocean plate moves

Volcano chain ▶

Magma breaks through the surface plate. As the plate moves, a new part moves over the hot spot. A new volcano forms and the old one dies.

ocean plate

hot spot

Magma temperature

1 Make sure the jar is clean and dry. Scoop out some margarine and drop it onto the bottom of the jar. For the best results, use solid margarine, rather than a soft margarine spread.

2 Pick up the jar and tilt it slightly. See what happens to the margarine. The answer is, not very much. It sticks to the bottom of the jar and does not slide down.

3 Fill the pitcher with hot water and pour some into the bowl. Shake it around to heat the bowl, then pour it out. Now pour the rest of the hot water into the bowl.

4 Pick up the jar and tilt it again. The margarine still will not move. Now place the jar on the bottom of the bowl. Keep your fingers clear of the hot water.

5 Start the stopwatch, and after one minute, take out the jar. Tilt it and see if the margarine moves. Return it to the bowl, and after another minute, look at it again.

6 Continue checking the jar for a few more minutes. After even a minute, the margarine will slide along the bottom as it warms and starts to melt. After several minutes, it is very fluid. Rocks in the upper mantle of the Earth react to heat in a similar way as the margerine.

Moving magma

The temperature of the rocks in the Earth's mantle can be as high as 2,700°F. At this temperature, the rocks would usually melt, but they are under such pressure from the rocks above them that they cannot melt completely. However they are able to flow slowly. This is rather like the solid piece of modeling material in the experiment below, which flows slightly when you put enough pressure on it. This kind of flow is called plastic flow. In places, the rocks in the upper part of the mantle do melt completely. This melted rock, called magma, collects in huge pockets called magma chambers. The magma rises because it is hotter and lighter than the semi-liquid rocks. Volcanoes form above magma chambers when the hot magma can rise to the surface. The second project demonstrates this principle using hot and cold water.

▲ **Surprise eruption**
Mount St Helens, in the north-east USA, lies in a mountain range that includes many volcanoes. Until 1980, Mount St Helens had not erupted in 130 years.

◄ **Flowing like rock**
Underneath the Earth's hard crust, the rock is semi-liquid and moves slowly. It flows in currents. Hot rock moves upward and cooler rock sinks down.

> YOU WILL NEED
>
> nonhardening modeling material,
>
> wooden board.

Plastic flow

1 Make sure that the table is protected by a sheet. Knead the lump of modeling material in your hands until it is soft and flexible. Make it into a ball and place on the table.

2 Place the board on top, and press it down. The modeling material flattens and squeezes out. It is just like semiliquid rock flowing under pressure. Make it into a ball again.

3 Press it with the board. Push the board forward at the same time. The modeling material will flow and allow the board to move forward like the plates in the Earth's crust.

Rising magma

1 Pour some of the food coloring into the small jar. You may need to add more later, to give your solution a deep color. This will make the last stage easier to see.

2 Fill the small pitcher with water from the hot tap. Pour it into the small jar. Fill it up to the brim, but don't let it overflow. Wipe off any water that spills down the sides.

Watch what happens. The colored hot water begins rising from the holes. This happens because the hot water is lighter, or less dense, than the cold water around it. Magma also rises because it is less dense than the semi-liquid rock surrounding it.

3 Cut a circular piece from the plastic food wrapping an inch or two bigger than the top of the small jar. Place it over the top and secure it with the rubber band.

4 With the sharp end of the pencil, carefully make two small holes in the plastic that is covering the top of the jar. If any colored water splashes out, wipe it off.

5 Now place the small jar inside the larger one. Use oven mitts because it is hot. Fill the large jug with cold water, and pour it into the large jar, not into the small one.

Erupting volcanoes

Volcanoes are places where molten (liquid) rock pushes up from below through splits in the Earth's crust. The word volcano comes from Vulcan, the name of the ancient Roman god of fire. Vulcanology is the term given to the study of volcanoes, and the scientists who study them are known as vulcanologists.

People usually think of volcanoes as producing molten rock. But volcanoes emit much more than just lava. The hot rock inside volcanoes produces many kinds of gases, such as steam and carbon dioxide. Some of these gases go into the air outside the volcano, and some are mixed with the lava that flows from it. The project opposite shows you how to make a volcano that throws out lava mixed with carbon dioxide. As you will see, the red, floury lava from your volcano comes out frothing, full of bubbles of this gas. In a real volcano, it is the gas that is mixed with the lava that makes the volcano suddenly explode.

▲ **Spectacular explosion**
This gigantic volcano has erupted with explosive violence. Huge clouds of rock and ash have been blasted into the air and rivers of red-hot lava cascade down its slopes. Explosive volcanoes have magma inside them that is full of gas. Gas bubbles swell inside the volcano and violently push out a mixture of lava and gas.

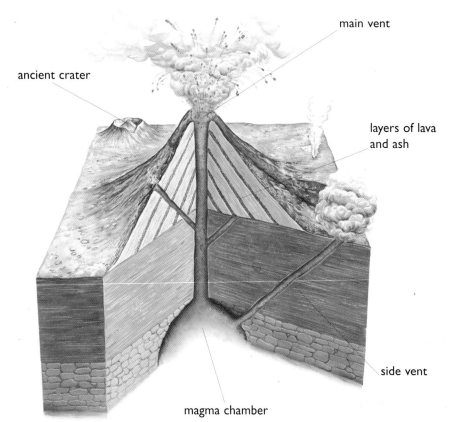

ancient crater

main vent

layers of lava and ash

side vent

magma chamber

◀ **Forming a cone**
When an explosive volcano erupts, magma (red-hot, molten rock) forces its way to the Earth's surface. It shoots into the air along with clouds of ash and gas, and runs out over the sides of the volcano. In time, layers of ash and lava build up to form a huge cone shape. Quiet volcanoes (those which do not explode because their magma contains very little gas) form a different shape.

Eruption

1 Make sure the pitcher is dry, or the mixture will stick to the sides. Empty the baking soda into the pitcher and add the flour. Mix the two thoroughly using the stirrer.

2 Place the funnel in the neck of the plastic bottle. Again, first make sure that the funnel is perfectly dry . Now pour the mixture of soda and flour from the pitcher.

3 Empty sand into the tray until it is half-full. Fill the pitcher with water and pour it into the tray to make the sand sticky, but not too wet. Mix together with the stirrer.

4 Stand the bottle containing the flour and soda mixture in the center of the plastic tray. Then start packing the wet sand around it. Pat the sand into a cone shape.

The sandy volcano you have made will begin to erupt. The vinegar and soda mix to give off carbon dioxide. This makes the flour turn frothy, and forces it out of the bottle as red lava.

5 Pour the vinegar into the pitcher. Then add enough food coloring to make the vinegar a rich, red color. White wine vinegar will make a richer color than malt vinegar.

6 Place the funnel in the mouth of the plastic bottle, and quickly pour into it the red-colored vinegar in the pitcher. Now remove the funnel from the bottle.

Volcanic shapes

Some parts of the world have ancient lava (molten rock) flows that are hundreds of miles long. Flows such as these have come from fissures (cracks) in the crust, which have poured out runny lava. This lava is much thinner than the lava produced by explosive volcanoes, which is sometimes called pasty lava. Scientists use the term viscosity to talk about how easily a liquid flows. Thin, runny liquids have a low viscosity, and thick liquids a high viscosity. The project shows the viscosities of two liquids, and how quickly they flow.

Heating solids to a sufficiently high temperature makes them melt and flow. Rock is no exception to this rule. Deep inside a volcano, hot rock becomes liquid and flows out on to the surface as lava. Its temperature can be as high as 2,200°F. Volcanoes grow in various shapes, depending on how runny or thick the lava is.

Submarine (undersea) volcanoes may grow in size until they rise above the surface of the sea.

Fissure volcanoes are giant cracks in the ground from which lava flows.

Shield volcanoes have runny lava and gentle slopes.

Vulcanian volcanoes produce thick, sticky lava and erupt with violent explosions.

Strombolian volcanoes spit out lava bombs in small explosions.

Plinian volcanoes produce thick, gassy lava and shoot columns of ash high into the air.

Lava viscosity

I Mark a large circle on each plate by drawing around the edge of a saucer. Pour a tablespoon of honey from the jar into the middle of one of the circles. Start the stopwatch.

2 After 30 seconds, mark with the pen how far the honey has run. After another 30 seconds mark again. Stop the watch when the honey has reached the circle.

3 Part-fill the pitcher with dish-washing detergent and pour middle into the centre of the other plate. Use the same amount as the honey you poured. Start the stopwatch.

After 30 seconds, note how far the liquid has run. You will probably find that it has already reached the circle. It flows faster because it has a much lower viscosity than honey.

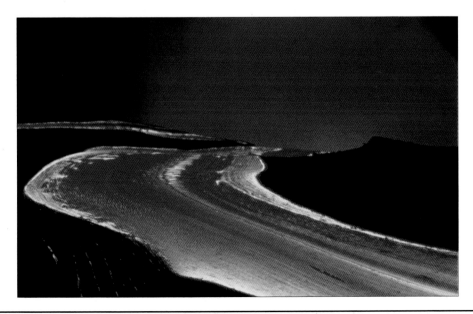

◀ **Fast-flowing river**

A river of molten lava flows down the slopes of the volcano Kilauea on the main island of Hawaii. Like the other volcanoes on the island, Kilauea is a shield volcano. It pours out very runny lava that flows for long distances, usually at speeds up to about 330 feet an hour. The fastest lava flows are called by their Hawaiian name of pahoehoe.

Vicious gases

The experiments here look at two effects that the gases given out by volcanoes can have. In the first project, you can see how the build up of gas pressure can inflate a balloon. If you have put too much gas-making mixture in the bottle, the balloon may explode. Be careful! When the gas pressure builds up inside a volcano, an enormous explosion takes place, often releasing a deadly, hot gas cloud.

Volcanoes often give out the gas carbon dioxide. This is heavier than air, so a cloud of carbon dioxide descends, pushing air out of the way. Carbon dioxide can kill people and animals. They suffocate, because the cloud of carbon dioxide has replaced the air, so oxygen cannot reach their lungs. The second project shows the effect of carbon dioxide. The candle needs oxygen to burn, just as we need it to breathe. Carbon dioxide replaces the air, so the candle goes out.

▲ **Blast off**

An enormous cloud of thick ash billows from the top of Mount St. Helens, in Washington. The volcano erupted on May 18, 1980. The ash cloud rose to a height of more than 12½ miles.

YOU WILL NEED
funnel, soft drink bottle, baking soda, vinegar, pitcher, balloon.

The balloon starts to blow up, because of the pressure, or force, of the gas in the bottle. The more gas there is, the more the balloon fills. Don't pop the balloon!

Gas pressure

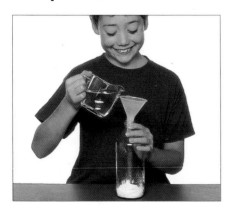

1 Place the funnel in the top of the bottle, and pour in some baking soda. Make sure the funnel is dry or the baking soda will stick to it. Pour the vinegar into the bottle using the funnel.

2 Remove the funnel. Quickly fit the neck of the balloon over the top of the bottle. Notice that the vinegar and soda are fizzing as they give off bubbles of gas.

Suffocating gas

1 Place the funnel in the bottle and add the baking soda. Pour the vinegar in from the pitcher. This bottle is your gas generator. The gas produced is carbon dioxide.

2 Knead a piece of modeling material until it is soft, then push it into the mouth of the bottle. Make sure it fits tightly. This will keep the gas from escaping.

3 Make a hole in the clay stopper with the pencil. Carefully push the straw through the hole, so that it hangs down into the bottle. Press the modeling material around the straw.

4 Stand both candles in the bottom of the large jar. Ask an adult to light them. Light the short one first, to avoid the danger of being burned if the tall candle were lit first.

5 Direct the straw of your gas generator into the bottom of the jar. Keep your arms well away from the candle flames. Soon you will find that the short candle goes out. The carbon dioxide gas has covered it and blocked out the oxygen that would have let it burn.

▲ A record of the past

Gas killed many of the victims at the Roman town of Pompeii. In A.D. 79 Pompeii was buried by avalanches of hot ash and rock from the erupting Vesuvius. Archaeologists have recreated the shapes of people and animals who died there. They filled hollows left by the bodies with wet plaster of Paris and let it harden. Then they removed the cast from the lava that had covered the bodies.

Steaming hot

In some places in the world, often near plate boundaries, there is magma (hot molten rock) very near to the Earth's surface. This causes other volcanic features such as geysers and hot springs, called geothermal features. The word comes from geo, meaning the Earth, and thermal, meaning heat.

Water from the Earth's surface trickles down through holes and cracks in the land. Geothermal features are almost always caused by magma that affect underground water.

The most spectacular geothermal feature is the geyser. This is a fountain of steam and water that erupts from holes in the ground. Vents (holes) called fumaroles, where steam escapes gently, are more common. Geysers and fumaroles may also give out carbon dioxide and sulfurous fumes.

Hot water can also mix with cooler water to create a hot spring, or with mud to form a bubbling mud hole. Water becomes heated in underground rocks to a temperature above body heat (about 98.6°F). Some hot springs can be twice this hot. Many are rich in minerals. For centuries, people have believed that bathing in these mineral-rich springs is good for health.

The first experiment on the opposite page shows you how to make a geyser using air pressure to force out water. Blowing into the top of the bottle increases the air pressure there. This forces the colored water out of the bottle through the long straw. In the second project, you can create a mud hole and discover the sort of bubbles that form in them.

> ### YOU WILL NEED
> **Geyser eruption:** nonhardening modeling material, 3 bendable straws, pitcher, food coloring, large plastic bottle, large jar.
> **Mudbaths:** cornflour, cocoa powder, mixing bowl, wooden spoon, measuring cup, milk, pan, oven mitt.

◄ Regular show

One of the most famous geysers in the world is Old Faithful, in Yellowstone National Park in Wyoming. This geyser erupts regularly about once every 45 minutes. Yellowstone is the most significant geothermal region in the USA. The National Park also boasts the world's tallest geyser, known as Steamboat. Its spouting column has been known to reach more than 380 feet.

Geyser eruption

1 Make two holes in a little ball of modeling material and push two bendable straws through it, as shown. Push another straw through the end of one of the first two straws.

2 Pour water into the pitcher and add the coloring. Then pour it into the bottle. Push the stopper into the neck, so that the elongated straw dips into the colored water.

3 Place the jar under the other end of the elongated straw, and blow into the other straw. Water spurts into the jar. If the long straw was upright, the water would spout upward like a geyser.

Mudbaths

1 Mix together two tablespoons of cornflour and two of cocoa powder in the bowl, using the wooden spoon. Stir the mixture thoroughly until it is an even color.

2 Pour about 10 fl oz of milk into the pan, and heat it slowly on a stove ring. Keep the ring on a low setting, to make sure the milk does not boil. Do not leave it unattended.

3 Add some cold milk, bit by bit, to the mixture of cornflour and cocoa in the bowl. Stir vigorously until the mixture has become a thick smooth cream.

4 Pour the creamy mixture into the hot milk in the pan. Hold the handle of the pan with the oven mitt, and stir to stop the liquid from sticking to the bottom of the pan.

5 If you have prepared your flour and cocoa mixture well, you will now have a smooth, hot liquid that looks something like liquid mud. Soon it will start sending up thick bubbles.

The thick bubbles in the mixture will pop with gentle, plopping sounds. This is exactly what happens in hot mud pools in volcanic areas.

Volcanic rocks

The lava that flows out of volcanoes eventually cools, hardens, and becomes solid rock. Different types of lava form different kinds of rocks.

In the first project, we see how keeping a liquid under pressure stops gas from escaping. The magma (molten rock) in volcanoes usually has a lot of gas dissolved in it. As it rises through the volcano, the gases start to expand. They help push the magma up and out if the vent is clear. If the vent is blocked, the gas pressure builds up and eventually causes the volcano to explode. The lava that comes from volcanoes with gassy magma forms rock-riddled with holes. In some explosive volcanoes, the lava contains so much gas that it forms pumice. This rock is so frothy and light that it floats on water.

When rising magma becomes trapped underground, it forces its way into gaps in the rocks and between the rock layers. This process is known as intrusion, and it is demonstrated by the second project. The rocks that form when the magma cools and solidifies are called intrusive rocks. Granite is the most common intrusive rock. Often, the heat of the intruding magma changes the surrounding rocks. They turn into metamorphic (changed form) rocks.

YOU WILL NEED
Dissolved gas: small jar with tight-fitting lid, bowl, pitcher, antacid tablets.
Igneous intrusions: plastic jar, bradawl, pieces of broken tiles, nonhardening modeling material, tube of colored toothpaste.

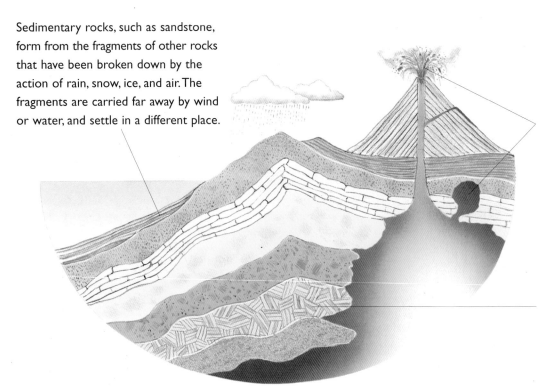

Sedimentary rocks, such as sandstone, form from the fragments of other rocks that have been broken down by the action of rain, snow, ice, and air. The fragments are carried far away by wind or water, and settle in a different place.

At some hot parts of the Earth beneath the crust, huge pockets of liquid rock (magma) form. The magma rises, cools, and solidifies to form igneous rocks such as granite. If magma reaches the surface of the Earth, it erupts as lava.

Within the Earth, the heat and pressure sometimes become so great that the surrounding rocks are changed. The new rocks are called metamorphic rocks. Marble is formed this way. It comes from limestone rock.

Dissolved gas

1 Stand the jar in the bowl. Pour cold water into the jar from the pitcher until the jar is nearly full to the top. Break up two antacid tablets and drop them into the jar.

2 Quickly screw the lid on the jar. Little bubbles will start to rise from the tablets, but will soon stop. Pressure has built up in the jar, and this prevents any more gas from escaping.

3 Now quickly unscrew the lid from the jar and see what happens. The whole jar starts fizzing. Removing the lid releases the pressure, and the gas in the liquid bubbles out.

Igneous intrusions

1 Make a hole in the bottom of the plastic jar with a bradawl, big enough to fit the neck of the toothpaste tube in. Keep your steadying hand away from the sharp end of the bradawl.

2 Place the pieces of broken tiles on the bottom of the jar. Keep them as flat as possible. They are supposed to represent the layers of rocks that are found in the Earth's crust.

3 Flatten out the modeling material into a disk as wide as the inside of the jar. Put the disk of modeling material inside the jar. Push it down firmly on top of the tiles.

4 Unscrew the top of the toothpaste tube, and force the neck into the hole you have made in the bottom of the bottle. You may have to widen it a little to get the neck in.

5 Squeeze the toothpaste tube. You will see the toothpaste pushing, or intruding, into the tile layers and making the disk on top rise. Molten magma often behaves in the same way. It intrudes into rock layers and makes the Earth's surface bulge.

Making crystals

Everything around you is made up of tiny particles called atoms. Crystals consist of atoms that are arranged in a regular repeating pattern. This gives the crystal its fixed outer shape. Most solid substances, including metals and minerals found in rocks, are in crystal form.

Igneous rocks are usually made of crystals that form as hot magma (molten rock) cools and solidifies. Crystals may also grow when a water solution containing minerals on the surface of the Earth evaporates. These two ways are demonstrated in the first two experiments.

The type of crystals that form depend on the substances that are dissolved in the liquid. Each mineral forms crystals with a characteristic shape. You can compare the crystals from the first two projects, which use two different solutions. The final experiment demonstrates how atoms are arranged in a crystal. In a liquid, the atoms are loosely joined together and can move around, which is why a liquid flows. As a liquid solidifies, the atoms join together in a regular pattern, like a pyramid, to form a crystal. When atoms are arranged in a disorderly way, they produce a gas.

▲ **Making crystals**

Place a drop of water on a small, dry mirror and then put it in the freezer. The water will freeze into crystals, which can be seen with a magnifying glass.

YOU WILL NEED
water, measuring cup, pan, sugar, tablespoon, wooden spoon, glass jar.

Growing crystals from sugar solution

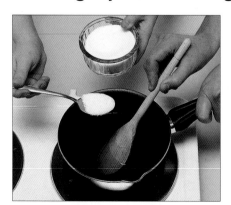

1 Ask an adult to heat a pint of water in a pan until it is hot, but not boiling. Using a tablespoon, add sugar to the hot water until no more sugar will dissolve in the solution.

2 Stir the solution well, then allow it to cool. When it is completely cold, pour the solution from the pan into a glass jar, and put it somewhere where it will not be disturbed.

After a few days or weeks, the solution starts to evaporate and the sugar in the solution will gradually begin to form crystals. The longer it is undisturbed, the larger your crystals will grow.

Growing crystals from sodium carbonate

1 Get an adult to pour about 1 cup of very hot water into a pitcher. Add a spoonful of sodium carbonate. Stir until it all dissolves. Add more sodium carbonate until no more will dissolve.

2 Dissolving a solid in a liquid makes a solution. Your solution is said to be saturated, because no more solid will dissolve. Pour the solution into a bowl, leaving undissolved solids in the pitcher.

3 A crystal needs somewhere to start growing. Use a piece of thread to attach the paper clip to the straw. The distance from straw to clip should be about two-thirds the depth of the bowl.

4 Balance the straw on top of the bowl to let the paper clip dangle in the water. As time goes by, water evaporates, leaving crystals on the paper clip.

5 After several days, remove the clip and crystals from the solution, and wash them under the cold tap. Look at the crystals through a magnifying glass. The shapes of your crystals are identical.

Make a model crystal

1 Fit a layer of blue marbles into the tray in a square pattern. Each central atom is surrounded by eight others. (In some substances, atoms are arranged in a hexagon—a six-sided shape.)

2 Add a second layer. Each marble sits in a dip between four marbles in the layer below. Add a third layer. Each marble is directly above a marble in the first layer.

3 Add two more layers of marbles to make up a complete model crystal. The model crystal you have made is the shape of a square pyramid, because you used a square tray.

Glass and bubbles

Igneous rocks begins deep within the Earth as magma (molten rock). The word igneous means "of fire". Magma rises toward the surface where it may erupt as lava from a volcano, or cool and solidify within the Earth's crust as igneous rock. Rocks formed in this way are a mass of interlocking crystals, which makes them very strong and ideal as building stones.

The size of the crystals in an igneous rock depends on how quickly the magma cooled. Lavas that cool quickly contain very small crystals. Basalt and andesite are two common kinds of fine-grained igneous rocks, with small crystals. Other rocks, such as granite, cooled more slowly because they solidified inside the Earth's crust. These have a grainy texture because the crystals had time to grow.

The experiments opposite show how igneous rocks can be grainy, or smooth and glassy. They use sugar to represent magma. Sugar melts at a low enough temperature for you to experiment with, but it will still be very hot, so ask an adult to help you do these projects. To make real magma, you would need to heat rock up to around 1,830°F until it melted! You can also make the sugar solution into bubbly honeycomb, a form similar to pumice stone.

▲ Basalt

Dark, heavy basalt is one of the most common volcanic rocks. It is formed from the thin, runny lava that pours out of some volcanoes. This sample is called vesicular basalt because it is riddled with vesicles (holes).

▲ Andesite

Lava from explosive volcanoes is thicker and less runny. It can form andesite, which is a lighter-colored rock than basalt. Andesite is so-called because it is the typical rock found in the Andes Mountains in Peru.

honeycomb (pumice)   toffee (obsidian)   fudge (granite)

▲ Pumice

The bubbles in honeycomb are like those in pumice. Pumice is a very light rock that is full of holes. It forms when lava that contains a lot of gas pours out of underwater volcanoes.

▲ Obsidian

Glassy toffee cools too rapidly to form crystals. Obsidian is a volcanic rock that is formed when lava cools very quickly. It looks like black glass and is often called volcanic glass.

▲ Granite

Fudge's grainy texture is similar to granite. The crystals are large, because they grew slowly as the magma cooled slowly. Rhyolite is a kind of granite with smaller crystals and sharp edges.

Crystalline rock

YOU WILL NEED

Crystalline rock: sugar, water, pan, safety glasses, wooden spoon, milk.

Glass and bubbles: waxed paper, butter, baking tray, oven mitt, sugar, water, pan, wooden spoon, safety glasses, baking soda.

1 Ask an adult to heat 2½ cups of sugar with a little water in a pan. Continue heating until the mixture turns brown, but not black, then add a splash of milk. Leave the mixture to cool.

2 After an hour, you should see tiny crystal grains in the fudge mixture. Once it is completely cool, feel its grainy texture in your hands. The texture is similar to granite.

Glass and bubbles

1 Use waxed paper to spread the butter on a metal baking tray. Put it in the freezer for at least an hour to get cold. Use oven mitts to take the tray from the freezer.

2 Ask an adult to heat about 2½ cups of sugar with a little water in a pan. The sugar dissolves in the water, but the water soon evaporates, leaving only sugar.

3 Stir the sugar mixture with a wooden spoon while it is heating. Make sure that the sugar does not burn and turn black. It should be golden brown.

4 Pour the mixture onto the cool baking tray. After 10 minutes, the glassy and brittle toffee will be cool enough to pick up. Like obsidian, toffee cools too rapidly to form crystals.

◄ Holey honeycomb
To make honeycomb, stir in a spoonful of baking soda in Step 3, just before you pour the sugar onto the tray. This will make tiny bubbles of gas in your "magma".

Layers on layers

Many of the most familiar rocks around us are sedimentary rocks. Particles of rock, shells, and bones of sea creatures settle in layers, and then harden into rock over thousands of years. Rock particles form when other rocks are eroded (worn down) by the weather and are carried away by wind, rivers, and ice sheets. They become sediments when they are dumped and settle. Sediments may collect in river deltas, lakes, and the sea. Large particles make conglomerates (large pebbles cemented together), medium-size ones make sandstones, and fine particles make clays.

To understand the processes by which sedimentary rocks are made, and how they form distinct layers called strata, you can make your own sedimentary rocks. Different strata of rock are laid down by different types of sediment, so the first project involves making strata using various things found in the kitchen. The powerful forces that move parts of the Earth's crust often cause strata to fold, fault, or just tilt, and you can see this, too. In the second project, you can make a type of sedimentary rock called a conglomerate, in which sand cements pebbles together.

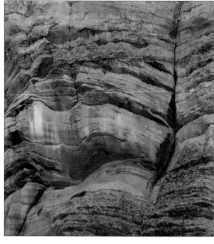

▲ **Cracks in the rockface**
Once they have formed, sedimentary rocks may be subject to powerful forces caused by the movement of the Earth's crust. Splits in the ground reveal how this strata has folded and cracked.

YOU WILL NEED

large jar, nonhardening modeling material, spoon, flour, kidney beans, brown sugar, rice, lentils (or a similar variety of ingredients of different colors and textures).

Your own strata

1 Press one edge of a large jar into a piece of modeling material, so that the jar sits at an angle. Slowly and carefully spoon a layer of flour about ¾in thick into the jar.

2 Carefully add layers of kidney beans, brown sugar, rice, lentils, and flour, building them up until they almost reach the top of the jar. Try to keep the side of the jar clean.

3 Remove the jar from the clay and stand it upright. The different colored and textured layers are like a section through a sequence of natural sedimentary rocks.

Making conglomerate rock

1 Put on a pair of rubber gloves. In an old plastic container, make up some plaster of Paris with water, following the instructions on the package. Stir with a fork or spoon.

2 Before the plaster starts to harden, mix some small pebbles, sand, and earth into the plaster of Paris. Stir the mixture thoroughly, to make sure it is all evenly distributed.

3 Leave the mixture for 10 minutes, until the plaster begins to harden, then take a small lump of it in your hand and mold it into a ball shape to look like conglomerate rock.

4 Make some more conglomerate rocks in different sizes with different amounts of pebbles in. Place the rocks on a spare piece of paper so that they can harden and dry out completely.

▲ Natural cement

Conglomerates in nature can be found in areas that were once under water. Small pebbles and shells become rounded and cemented together by the water.

◄ Clues in the cutaway

The one-mile deep Grand Canyon, in Arizona, was cut by the Colorado River. The cliff face reveals colorful strata (layers of rock). The strata at the bottom are more than two billion years old. Those at the top are about 60 million years old. Each layer is a different type of rock, suggesting that conditions in this region changed many times in the past. For this reason, sedimentary rock strata can provide valuable clues about the distant history of the Earth.

What's a fossil?

The remains of some plants and animals that died long ago can be seen in rock as fossils. After an animal dies, it may become buried in sediments—rock particles ground down by wind and water. Slowly, over thousands of years, the sediments compact together to form sedimentary rock. The shape or outline of the plant or animal is preserved.

The study of fossils, called palaeontology, tells us much about how life evolved, both in the sea and on the land. Fossils give clues to the type of environment in which an organism lived, and can also help to date rocks.

These projects will help you to understand how two types of fossil came to exist. One type forms when sediment settles around a dead animal or plant. It hardens to rock, and the plant or animal rots away. This space in the rock is an outline of the dead animal or plant. This is usually how the soft parts of an animal, or a delicate leaf, are preserved. You can make this kind of fossil using a shell. In this case the shell does not decay—you simply remove it from the plaster.

The second project shows you another kind of fossil. Here, the skeleton of a decaying animal is filled with minerals. The minerals gradually become rock. This gives a solid fossil that is a copy of the original body part.

fern

ammonite

▲ Turned to stone

Two common fossils are shown here. Fossils of sea creatures are often found, because their bodies cannot decay completely underwater. Ammonites were hard-shelled sea creatures that lived between 60 million and 400 million years ago. Fernlike fossils are often found in coal.

YOU WILL NEED

Fossil imprint: safety glasses, plastic container, plaster of Paris, water, fork, strip of paper, paper clip, nonhardening modeling material, shell, wooden board, hammer, chisel.

Solid fossil: spare paper, rolling pin, modeling material, shell, petroleum jelly, paper clip, strip of paper, glass jar, plaster of Paris, water, fork.

How fossils are formed

An animal or plant dies. Its body falls onto the sand at the bottom of the ocean, or into mud on land. If it is buried quickly, then the body is protected from being eaten.

The soft parts of the body rot away, but the bones and teeth remain. After a long time, the hard parts are replaced by minerals—usually calcite, but sometimes pyrite or quartz.

After millions of years, the rocks in which the fossils formed are eroded and exposed again. Some fossils look as fresh now as the day when the plant or animal was first buried.

Fossil imprint

1 In a plastic container, mix up the plaster of Paris with some water. Follow the instructions on the package. Make sure the mixture is fairly firm and not too runny.

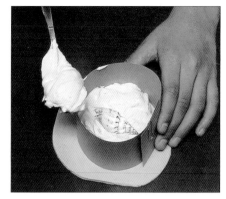

2 Make a collar out of a strip of paper fastened with a paper clip. Use modeling material to make a base to fit under the collar. Press the shell into the clay. Surround the shell with plaster.

3 Leave your plaster rock to dry for at least half an hour. Crack open the rock and remove the shell. You will then see the imprint left behind after the shell has gone.

Solid fossil

1 Put a spare piece of paper down on your work surface to protect it. Using the rolling pin, roll out some modeling material into a flat circle, roughly ¾in thick.

2 Press your shell, or another object with a distinctive shape, deep into the clay to leave a clear impression. Do not press it all the way to the paper at the bottom.

3 Remove the shell and lightly rub some petroleum jelly over the clay circle, which is now the shell mold. This will help you to remove the plaster fossil later.

4 Use the paper clip to fasten the paper strip into a collar for the mould. Mix up some plaster of Paris according to the instructions, pour it in, and leave it to set for half an hour.

5 Remove the solid plaster from the mold. In order not to damage them, palaeontologists have to remove fossilized bones or teeth, from rock or earth, very carefully.

These are the finished results of the two projects. Real fossils are imprints of organisms that lived millions of years ago.

Hard as nails!

The best way to learn about rocks is to look closely at as many different types as you can find. Look at pebbles on the beach and the stones in your garden. You will find that they are not all the same. Collect specimens of different pebbles and compare them. Give each stone an identification number and record where you found it, and its characteristics. A magnifying glass will help you see more details than can be seen with the naked eye. Look for different colors, shapes, and hardness. Ask an adult to take you to a geological museum to compare your stone with the specimens there.

You can try simple versions of tests that geologists use, on the following pages. They will help you identify some samples that you have collected. The first test involves rubbing a rock onto the back of a tile to leave a streak mark. The color of the streak can give a clue to what minerals are present in the rock. The second test shows you how to discover a rock's hardness, by seeing how easily a mineral scratches. Hardness is measured on a scale devised in 1822 by Friedrich Mohs. He made a list of ten common minerals called Mohs' scale, which runs from 1 (the softest) to 10 (the hardest). The hardest natural mineral is diamond, with a hardness of 10. It will scratch all other minerals.

▲ Be a detective

Clean a rock with a stiff brush and water. Stand in plenty of light and experiment to find the correct distance to see the rock's details clearly with a magnifying glass.

beach pebbles

▲ Wearing away

Look at the different sizes of pebbles on a beach. The constant to-and-fro of the waves grinds the pebbles smaller and smaller. Eventually these particles will form sedimentary rock.

quartz

copper

▲ What is a mineral?

All rocks are made up of one or more minerals. Minerals, such as copper and quartz, are natural, solid, nonliving substances. Each mineral has definite characteristics, such as shape and color, that distinguish it from other minerals.

◀ Hidden inside

When mineral-rich water fills a crack or cavity in a rock, veins and geodes form. A geode is a rounded rock, with a hollow center lined with crystals. The beautiful crystal lining is revealed when it is split open. Geodes are highly prized by mineral collectors.

outside of geode

inside of geode

Streak test

1 Place a tile face down, so that the rough side is facing upward. Choose one of your samples and rub it against the tile. You should see a streak of color appear on the tile.

2 Make streaks using the other samples and compare the colors. Rocks made of several minerals may leave several colored streaks. Try to identify them in your field guide.

Testing for hardness

1 Clean some rock samples with water using a nail brush. Scratch the rocks together. On the Mohs' scale, a mineral is harder than any minerals it can make scratches on.

2 A fingernail has a hardness of just over 2. Scratch each rock with a fingernail—if it scratches the rock, the minerals out of which the rock is made have a hardness of 2 or less.

3 Put aside those rocks scratched by a fingernail. Scratch those remaining with a coin. A coin has a hardness of about 3, so minerals it scratches are less than 3.

4 Now scratch the remaining rocks on a glass jar. If any of the rocks make a scratch on the jar, then the minerals they contain must be harder than glass.

5 Put aside any rocks that will not scratch the glass. They are less hard than glass, which measures somewhere between 5 and 6. Try scratching the remainder of the rocks with a steel file (hardness 7), and finally with a sheet of sandpaper (hardness 8).

Testing for minerals

Rocks and minerals are the naturally occurring materials that make up planet Earth. Rocks are used for buildings, and many minerals are prized as jewels. Most people think of rocks as hard and heavy, but soft materials, such as sand, chalk, and clay, are also considered to be rocks. Different rocks are made up from mixtures of different minerals. The minerals inside a rock form small crystals that are locked together to form a hard solid.

Geologists (scientists who study the Earth and its rocks) use many different methods to identify minerals that make up rocks. These experiments will help you to discover which minerals are in a rock sample. You can also identify rocks with a magnifying glass or from their hardness.

The acid test demonstrates if a gas is given off by the mineral. The second experiment is used to discover a rock sample's specific gravity. It compares a mineral's density to the density of water. Density measures how compact the particles are that make up a sample. Every mineral has a different density, which means that samples of the same mineral will have the same density.

▲ **Weighing up the evidence**
These two bricks are the same size and shape, but do not weigh the same. The materials they are made of have different densities.

YOU WILL NEED

vinegar, bowl, spoon, samples of

different stones, magnifying glass,

reference book.

Acid test

1 Pour some vinegar into a bowl. Drop rock samples into the vinegar. If gas bubbles form, then the rock contains minerals called carbonates (such as calcite).

2 Alternatively, you can put a few drops of vinegar on each rock sample. Watch them carefully for clues to what they might be. Chalk, marble and limestone make vinegar fizz.

3 Limestone reacts with vinegar. Like chalk and marble, it reacts because it is a type of calcium carbonate. Common rocks such as flint, granite, and sandstone are unaffected.

What is in soil?

1 Put on a pair of gardening gloves and place a trowel full of soil into the sieve. Shake the sieve over a piece of paper for about a minute or so.

2 Tap the side of the sieve gently, to help separate the different parts of the soil. Are there chunks that will not go through the sieve? Can you see if any of the chunks are rock?

3 Use a magnifying glass to examine the soil particles that fall onto the paper. Are there any small creatures or mineral grains? Make a note of what you see in your notebook.

Big or small?

YOU WILL NEED

Wormery: large and small plastic bottles, scissors, funnel, gloves, damp soil, sand, six worms, rotting leaves, black paper, sticky tape.

What is in soil?: gloves, trowel, soil, sieve, paper, magnifying glass, notebook, pen.

Big or small?: scissors, large clear plastic bottle, wooden spoon, gravel, earth, sand, water, pitcher.

---

1 Use a pair of scissors to cut the top off a large, clear plastic bottle. Ask an adult to help, if you need to. You can throw away the top part of the bottle.

floating soil and plant fragments

water made cloudy by fine particles of clay

settled mineral particles

2 Use a spoon to scoop some gravel, earth, and sand into the bottom of the bottle. Add water to the mixture, until it nearly reaches to the top of the bottle.

3 Stir vigorously to mix the stones, earth, and sand with the water. In a river, soil and rock particles are mixed together and carried along by the moving water.

Leave the mixture to settle. You should find that the particles settle into different layers, with the heaviest particles at the bottom, and the lightest at the top.

71

Examining soil

Beneath the ground, the soil teems with life. Worms, slugs, millipedes, and beetles live there, feeding on decaying matter. Tiny living creatures, called decomposers, break down everything that remains. Decomposers include microscopic bacteria, fungi, woodlice, mites, and small insects. They digest organic material such as dead animals, leaves, and plants, and break it down into nutrients. This process, called decomposition, creates a rich fertilizer for plants growing in the soil. As organic material rots, its nutrients or goodness are returned to the soil. The nutrients dissolve in rain water, and trickle down to tree and other plant roots below.

The first experiment demonstrates the best conditions for decomposing plants. It shows that plant material decays quickest in warm, moist areas. You can take a closer look at the decomposers themselves in the second project, which shows how to separate creepy-crawlies from the rotting leaves they live in. You could repeat the experiment with leaves from a different area, and see if the insects you find are the same.

▲ Feast for woodlice

Rotting, in nature, does not happen by itself. Dead leaves are food for decomposers, such as woodlice. They eat the fallen leaves and pass many of the nutrients back into the soil, to be taken up again by the trees' roots.

Watching decay in the soil

YOU WILL NEED
gardening gloves, trowel (optional), two clean plastic containers, soil, dead leaves, water in a watering can, one container lid.

1 Be sure to wear a pair of rubber gloves for this project. Use your hand, or a trowel if you prefer, to fill two plastic containers with plenty of dry soil.

2 Put a layer of dead leaves on top of the soil in one of the containers. Water the leaves and soil thoroughly, then press the lid onto the container to cover it.

3 Place a layer of leaves on the dry soil in the other container. Do not water it and do not cover the container. Store both containers in a dry place.

After a few weeks, the leaves in the wet soil (*above left*) will have begun to rot, and those in the dry soil (*above right*) will have shrivelled.

Studying decomposers

YOU WILL NEED

plastic funnel, large clear jar, gloves, rotting leaves from a compost heap, black paper, sticky tape, desk lamp, magnifying glass, field guide.

1 Rotting leaves are covered in insects and other creepy-crawlies. You can separate them by using a lamp, a funnel, and a large jar. Put the funnel inside the jar, as shown.

2 Wearing a pair of gardening gloves, loosely fill the funnel with rotting leaves. Tape a sheet of black paper around the sides of the jar to block out the light.

3 Place the lamp so that it shines on the leaves. The creatures will move away from the heat and the light of the lamp, and fall down the slippery funnel into the jar below.

After an hour, there will be several creatures in the jar. Look at them with a magnifying glass and use a field guide to identify them. Then return the creatures to where you found them.

Tree study

There are several kinds of trees. In tropical rainforests, where it is warm and wet all year, most trees are evergreen and keep their leaves the entire year. Tropical rainforests are found near the Equator, where there is little difference between the seasons. In countries with a temperate (moderate) climate, deciduous, broad-leaved trees shed their leaves in autumn. Losing leaves reduces evaporation. This helps the tree conserve energy and water when the ground water is frozen, and reduces damage by frost.

Trees can be identified by looking at such characteristics as bark, leaves, and flowers, and in autumn by their fruits and nuts, some of which are shown on the right. The size and shape of the trunk and branches can also help to identify a tree, and scientists record the tree's girth by measuring the distance around the trunk at chest height. You can study trees in your backyard, a local park or the wood following the same checks. Choose an area of mixed woodland with many different trees. Always take an adult with you to keep you safe.

leaf from a plane tree

seedcase from a sycamore tree

hips and leaves from a cockspur thorn tree

seeds from a lime tree

a chestnut and its case from a horse chestnut tree

acorn and its cup from an oak tree

Identifying trees

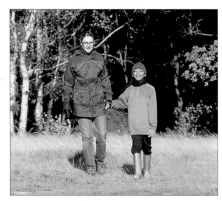

1 Walk along a path in a park or in the woods. Try to identify the trees you find there from their general height and shape. Use a field guide on trees to help you.

2 Bark can help you identify some trees. Silver birch bark is smooth and white with dark cracks. Match the bark of different trees with pictures in your guide.

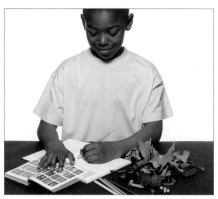

3 Study leaf colors and shapes, and the fruits and seeds of trees. Learn to identify trees with the help of the field guide, and make a record of them in a notebook.

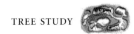

Measuring a tree's height

1 With the yardstick, measure 19 yds from the tree and push the stick into the ground. Measure another yard from the stick and lie down straight on the ground.

2 Use one eye to line up the top of the tree with the stick. Get a friend to mark this point on the stick in the ground. The height of the tree is 20 times this distance.

Measuring a tree's girth

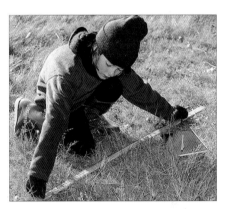

1 Stick a piece of tape on the end of a piece of string. Wrap the string around a tree trunk at chest height. Mark where it meets the tape with your finger.

2 Lay the string along the yardstick to find the length. This number is the girth of the tree. Measure another tree of the same species. Is its girth the same? Why might they differ?

> 1 square = 2.5cm
> evergreen
> beech
> horse chesnut
> cherry
> silverbirch

3 Make a chart with drawings of the different trees that you have measured. The trees with the thickest trunks are usually older than those with slender trunks.

▲ Rings of age

You can clearly see the growth rings on the trunk of this old oak tree. Each year, the tree grows a new ring of wood just under the bark.

Looking at bark

▲ **Close-up view**

If you look closely at the bark of a tree, you can discover many clues about its life. Plants and fungi may be clinging to the surface. There might also be insects and other tiny creatures hiding inside cracks...

YOU WILL NEED

magnifying glass, field guide,

notebook, pencil.

Become a bark detective

The skin that covers a tree—the bark—keeps the tree from drying out and helps to protect it against attack by animals and fungi. Bark may be thin and smooth, or thick and knobbly, depending on the type of tree and its age. Young trees usually have smooth bark on their trunks and branches. Old bark stretches and cracks or peels, as the trunk grows wider year by year. Just underneath the bark is a delicate layer of tissue called a phloem. It carries nutrients from the leaves to all parts of the tree. If a bark is damaged all around the tree trunk, the flow of food stops and the tree dies.

The appearance of the bark can help you decide what species (type) a tree is. Different trees have different kinds of bark. A mature beech tree has smooth, thin bark that is about ½in deep. A redwood tree of the same size has hairy, fibrous bark that is up to 6in thick. Many conifers, such as pines and spruces, have bark that flakes off. Follow the first two projects and become a bark detective, by studying the bark up close and making a collection of your own bark rubbings. The third project will help you estimate the size of a tree.

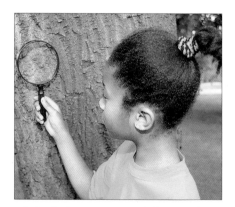

1 Bark does not stretch, but cracks and peels as a tree grows. Use a magnifying glass to search in the cracks during the spring and summer for tiny insects and other creatures.

2 The bark has fallen away from this dead tree, revealing the holes chewed by beetle grubs underneath. Some grubs live under the bark for several years.

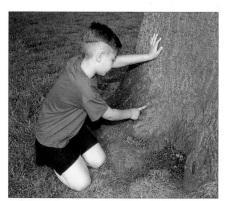

3 Where the bark is damp, you will often find powdery green patches. These are millions of microscopic plants called algae, which live side by side on the bark's surface.

Bark rubbing book

YOU WILL NEED

paper, wax crayons, pencil, colored
card, bradawl or hole puncher,
ribbon, adhesive.

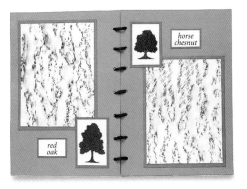

1 Ask a friend to hold a sheet of
paper steady against the bark. Rub
the side of a crayon over the paper
with long, even strokes. Write the
name of the tree beside each rubbing.

2 Punch holes into pieces of colored
card and bind them together
with ribbon. Stick your rubbings on
to each page. You could include
a silhouette of each tree, too.

Measuring the crown

YOU WILL NEED

compass, marker, yardstick,

graph paper, ruler,

colored pencils

1 Using the compass, walk away from
the tree toward north. Ask a friend
to call out when you reach the edge of
the area covered by the leaves. Place a
marker at this point.

2 Repeat for the other seven main
compass directions (NE, E, SE, S,
SW, W, NW). Measure the distances
back to the trunk with a yard stick and
note them down.

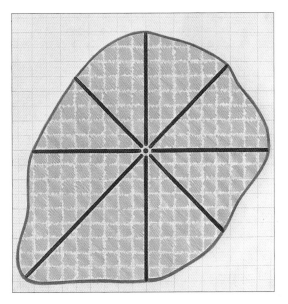

3 Plot your results on a piece of
graph paper. Measure ½in on the
paper for each yard on the ground.
Draw lines from the centre of the
paper, for each compass direction.

What you have sketched and
coloured in shows the shape
of the area covered by trees
leaves and branches (the
crown). Count the squares
and half squares to find the
size of the area of the crown.
Do not count part-squares if
they are less than a half. Each
½in square represents 1 yard.
Compare with other trees in
the area. Generally, the older
the tree, the more likely it
will have a larger crown.

Specimen collection

Different kinds of trees grow naturally in different parts of the world. Where they grow depends mainly on climate. Look closely at trees in winter, and you will see that even deciduous trees are not completely bare. Each twig has buds along its sides and at the tip. Buds have protective skins with tiny immature leaves and stems curled up inside. When spring sunshine warms the trees, buds begin to grow and swell. Finally, they burst open and small leaves emerge. Leaves contain pipes called veins. Water pumps into these veins, making the leaves stiffen and flatten as they grow to full size.

To learn about trees, you can make a collection of dead leaves, cones, and bark from each one you study. Do not forget to look for things throughout the year— flowers and buds in spring, seeds and fruit in the fall. Label your collection.

YOU WILL NEED

tree specimens (leaves, cones, bark chips), heavy books, kitchen paper, glue, notebook, field guide, magnifying glass, shoe box, pieces of card.

bud scale folded leaf short stem

▲ Budding

Buds grow in the center of a twig between two leaf stems. An unopened bud contains tiny leaves, and a shoot that will grow in spring and make the leaf stem longer. The illustration above shows what it looks like inside.

Tree zones

Evergreen conifer trees, such as pine and firs, usually grow where the climate is cold. Long, snowy winters are followed by short, cool summers, with moderate amounts of rain. Forests of conifers grow in a band across North America, Europe, and Asia.

Broad-leaved deciduous trees, such as oak, ash, and maple, grow in temperate climates away from hot, dry tropics or the snowy poles. There are more kinds of trees than in a coniferous forest. Temperate forests are found in North America, Europe, Asia, and New Zealand.

Tropical countries lie close to the Equator. The weather is hot, and daylight lasts for 12 hours a day for most of the year. Dense rainforests grow where heavy rain falls almost continuously, such as South America, Africa, Asia, and Australasia.

Savanna is a dry, tropical grassland, with some shrubs and bushes. Trees grow alone, or in widely spaced small groups. Forests cannot grow because the dry season lasts most of the year. Trees that do grow here are species that can survive for long periods without water.

Collecting specimens

1 How many different leaves and cones can you find? Make sure you note down the name of the tree that each specimen comes from. Start a collection with your friends.

2 To dry and flatten your leaves, place sheets of kitchen paper between the pages of a large and heavy book. Lay your leaves out on the paper on one side only. Close the book.

3 Pile more books on top. Make sure the pile cannot topple over and will not get disturbed. The weight presses the leaves flat, and the kitchen paper absorbs moisture.

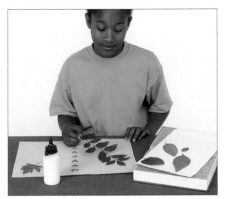

4 Wait for at least one month, until the leaves are flat and dry. Glue them into your notebook, or onto sheets of thick paper, and make them into a book. Use a field guide to identify each leaf.

5 For bark specimens, only collect bark from dead trees that have fallen over. You can make bark rubbings from living trees. See page 76 for instructions on how to make rubbings.

6 Springtime flowers soon wither and die. These young horse chestnuts will last much longer. It is better to take photographs of flowers, rather than pick them.

7 You can look at young cones and leaves from the lowest branches of evergreen pines, firs, and cedars. Look under these trees for cones that have fallen.

Make a large display case for your collection. You can make this from a shoe box by sticking in pieces of card to make compartments. Pressed leaves keep their shape and can last for a long time, if they are kept dry.

How plants grow

All plants need water to live. They do not take in food as animals do, but make their own using water from the ground, and carbon dioxide gas from the air. Water is absorbed through a plant's roots. It travels up through the stem or trunk into the leaves, shoots, and flowers. The water also carries the nutrients from the soil to all parts of the plant. In the leaves, nutrients and water are used for photosynthesis, the process of making energy from light. Excess water not needed by the plant evaporates back into the air in the form of water vapor in a process called transpiration. You can see how much water vapor is transpired by a plant in the first experiment.

When a seed begins to grow, we say that it has germinated. Germination occurs when conditions are warm and moist enough for the seed to swell and split its skin. A tiny root grows downward, and a thin shoot pushes upward toward the light. The second project shows you how to germinate a seed and help it grow into a tree. Germinating a seed in this way takes about two months.

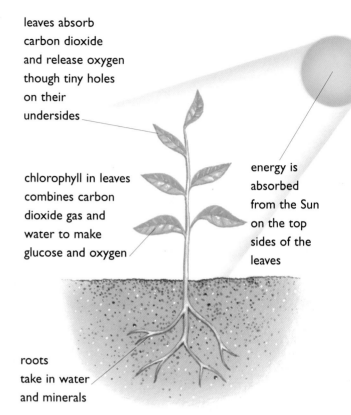

leaves absorb carbon dioxide and release oxygen though tiny holes on their undersides

chlorophyll in leaves combines carbon dioxide gas and water to make glucose and oxygen

energy is absorbed from the Sun on the top sides of the leaves

roots take in water and minerals

▲ Converting energy

Photosynthesis is the process through which plants use the water in the ground and the energy in sunlight to make their food. Leaves take in carbon dioxide and water to make oxygen and glucose (sugar). Glucose flows to all parts of the plant, supplying energy for growth. Oxygen gas escapes through the holes on the underside of the leaves. The oxygen is released back into the air. We need oxygen to breathe.

Survival in the wetlands ▶

Swamps are places where the ground is permanently waterlogged, such as in muddy river estuaries. Most trees cannot survive in swamps, because they need fresh water and air around their roots. Some types of mangroves have breathing roots that grow upward, so that their tips are above the surface of the water. Mangrove swamps are home to kingfishers, giant water bugs, crabs, turtles, crocodiles, and mudskippers, a type of fish that spends much of its time out of water.

Evaporation in action

1 Water the house plant well using a watering can. Water the plant at the base, so the roots can draw the water up. If you water the plant from the top, water just the soil, not the plant itself.

2 Place a large, transparent plastic bag over the plant, taking care not to damage the leaves. Tape the bag tightly around the pot. Leave the plant overnight.

◀ Floating water

Trees pass millions of gallons of water vapor into the air each day. The vapour forms thick clouds of tiny water droplets over the forest.

3 Look at the plant the next day. Inside the bag, water vapor given off by the plant turns back into water. The air inside is warm and moist, like the air in a rainforest.

Germinate an acorn

1 Fill the flower pot with compost and bury an acorn just beneath the surface. Put it in a warm place and keep the soil moist. Plant several acorns, since one may not germinate.

2 When a tiny tree starts to grow by itself, it is called a seedling. It needs light and regular watering to grow well. Do not soak the soil with water, or the roots will rot and die.

3 Your seedling should grow rapidly for a few weeks and then stop. During the winter, it will need little water. In the spring, you can take the seedling out of its pot and plant it outside.

Reaching for light

Look at a leaf and you will see that the top side is usually greener than the underside. This is because there is more chlorophyll, a green substance that traps energy from sunlight. Plants cannot move around to find food as animals do. Instead, they make their own. The green cells work like tiny solar panels, using sunlight to combine carbon dioxide gas from the air and water from the ground. The cells then produce a sugar (glucose) and oxygen gas. This process is called photosynthesis. Without light, plants cannot make their food.

Photosynthesis is the ultimate source of food on Earth, because animals eat plants or other animals that live on plants. Photosynthesis is also the source of all oxygen in our atmosphere. The projects show how plants try to reach the light. Epiphytes special kinds of plants that do not need to grow in soil. They live on high branches in the rainforests to get closer to the light.

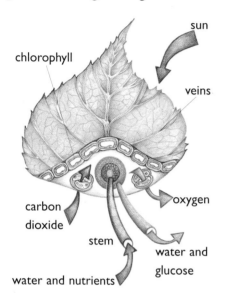

chlorophyll

sun

veins

carbon dioxide

oxygen

stem

water and glucose

water and nutrients

▲ **Making energy**
Photosynthesis happens near the top surface of a leaf, where sunlight has the strongest impact.

▲ **Catching the rays**
Trees spread their leaves widely to absorb as much energy as they can from sunlight. They use the energy to make a sugary substance called glucose. Liquids flow in and out of leaves through veins. Veins also act like ribs that help to stiffen the leaf and keep it flat.

Grow your own epiphyte

1 Put on a pair of gloves to protect your hands. Wrap moss around one end of the branch or a piece of driftwood. Tie the moss securely in place with thread.

2 Pile some gravel into a sturdy plant pot, until the pot is almost full. It needs to be almost full to support the wood. You could use a trowel to help you transfer the gravel.

3 Now push the branch or driftwood down into the gravel, until it stands up in the pot without tipping it over. Use a water spray to spray the moss with water.

4 Arrange the epiphytes (available from garden stores) by pressing them gently into the moss. A drop of glue on the base of each plant will help to hold it in place.

5 Remember to spray the epiphytes from time to time with water. You could also add a few drops of liquid plant food, to help the epiphytes to grow.

Epiphytes grow well indoors and make an unusual display. They do not need soil to grow. Instead they wrap their roots around a branch.

Searching for the light

YOU WILL NEED

Grow your own epiphyte: garden gloves, sphagnum moss, branch or drfitwood, thread, gravel, plant pot, trowel, water spray, epiphytes, glue, liquid plant food.

Searching for the light: shoe box, scissors, stiff card, tape, black paint, paintbrush, garden gloves, runner bean, plant pot, compost, water.

1 Watch a plant search for the light as it grows, by making a maze. Cut a hole in the end of a shoe box and stick eight flaps of card inside with tape, as shown here.

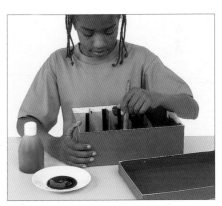

2 Paint the inside of the box and lid black all over. The black paint will stop the light that enters through the hole from being reflected around inside the box.

3 Wearing gloves, plant a runner bean in a small pot of compost. Water the soil each day to keep it moist, but not too wet. On some days, no water may be needed.

4 When the plant has a shoot, stand it at the bottom of your maze. Close the lid and place the maze in a sunny spot. Once a day, remove the lid to see if the seedling needs watering.

The plant will find its way through the maze as it steadily moves toward the light. Eventually, it will poke out through the hole at the top of the shoe box.

Natural water pumps

When you look at a tree, you only see a part of it. Unseen roots spread out underground as wide as the branches above. These roots anchor a tree in the ground and hold it up against the force of the wind. Roots also help the tree to grow, by taking up water and nutrients from the soil through the trunk to the leaves. Trees act like a natural pump—many trees over 165 feet tall pump hundreds of gallons of water a day in order to grow. You can suck a drink up through a straw, but trees cannot do this. They use a method called osmosis to draw the water upward. The first experiment shows how osmosis works. Water inside the roots (sap) has a higher concentration of sugar than the water outside. The process of osmosis draws water from the soil, where the concentration is low, to inside the root, where concentration is high.

The second experiment uses coloured water to show how water actually travels up a plant's root. All living things are made up of little units called cells. Water can travel through cell walls but sugars cannot. During osmosis, water always moves in a set direction – from the side where there is less sugar dissolved in it to the side where there is more.

▲ **Suck it and see**
To find out how difficult it is to suck up water, carefully tape together straws with tape. The longer the straw, the more difficult it is for you to suck up the drink. The best mechanical pumps can only manage 30 feet.

How osmosis works

> ### YOU WILL NEED
>
> large potato, ruler, chopping board, peeler, knife, teaspoon, two shallow dishes, water, sugar.

1 You will need a large, smooth potato about 4in long and 2 ½in across. Carefully peel the potato on a chopping board to protect the work surface.

2 Cut the peeled potato in half, and then slice off the rounded ends. You will now have two round potato slices. Each slice should be about 1½in thick.

3 Use a teaspoon to scoop out a hollow in each potato slice. Place each slice in its own shallow dish and fill the dishes with water to about 1½in in depth.

4 Half fill both hollows with water. Add ½ tsp of sugar to one hollow. Cover and leave the potatoes for one day. (*Dye has been added to the water here to make it show up.*)

5 The level of liquid in the sugary hollow has risen. Osmosis has made more water move into this potato from the dish. The level in the other potato has not risen.

Osmosis in color

YOU WILL NEED

water, two tall drinking glasses, water-soluble ink or food dye, white carnation, scissors, tape.

1 Pour some water into two tall drinking glasses. Add a few drops of ink or food dye to one of the glasses to give the water a strong, bright color.

2 Use scissors to split the stem of the carnation lengthwise to about half way up the stem. Bind the stem with tape, so that it does not split any further.

3 Place the glasses side by side on a window sill, and stand one half of the stem in each glass. Lean the flower against the window if it will not stand up on its own.

4 After a few hours, check to see what has happened. One half of the flower will be colored with the dye. The other half of the flower will have remained white.

Colored water is drawn up one side of the split stem. The petals on that side of the flower have turned pink.

Seeds and plant life

Most plants reproduce by making seeds, which sprout and grow into new plants. To produce seeds, plants must be fertilized by pollen, usually from another plant of the same species (kind). Many plants rely on insects, such as bees and butterflies, to spread pollen. Seeds are mostly spread by animals that eat the fruit produced by plants, and by the wind. In some plants, such as those in rainforests, seeds may also be carried by water. The plants in your local area disperse (spread) their seeds in these ways, too. In the company of an adult, you can survey the seeds and plants in the local woods.

YOU WILL NEED

eight pegs, yardstick or tape measure, string, field guide, pen, notebook, colored pencils and pens, graph paper.

Performing out a plant survey

1 Choose a patch of ground to sample and put in a peg. Measure 1 yard with the ruler, and put in another peg. Stretch and tie a piece of string between the pegs.

2 Now measure the remaining sides, pushing in two more pegs and stretching and tying string between them to mark out one square yard.

3 Measure and mark the midpoint of each piece of stretched string with pegs. Stretch more string between these pegs to divide the square into quarters.

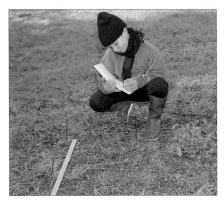

4 Use your field guide to help you to identify the plant species growing in each quarter of the square. Do different plants, or the same ones, grow in each area?

5 Draw a chart on graph paper to record each plant's position. Use different colors for each plant type that you found. Add up the total number of each type of plant.

Looking at seed dispersal

YOU WILL NEED

field guide, collecting pot, muslin, rubber band, notebook, pencil, colored pencils.

1 Look for nibbled nuts and acorns. These seeds provide food for many animals. Collect seeds in a pot, cover them with muslin and secure with a rubber band.

2 Visit your local pond or stream to find seeds, such as alders, that are dispersed by water. Use your field guide to identify any seeds you see floating on the water.

3 Maple and sycamore trees have light seeds with wings. As they fall, the wings spin the seed through the air, helping it to fly farther and germinate far from the parent tree.

4 Find a dandelion head. Plants such as dandelions have very light seeds, each with its own small parachute of fine threads. These are carried away by the wind.

5 Look for the seed capsules of poppies. They are like pepper shakers with hundreds of tiny seeds inside. As the wind shakes the capsule, the seeds pop out and scatter widely.

When you walk through long grass, you may find burrs—fruits with tiny hooks—stuck on to your coat or to a pet's fur. Draw pictures of all the seeds and fruits that you find. Color and label them.

Growing from fruit

There are many kinds of fruits grown in the garden. Some fruits are soft, such as apples and oranges, and others are hard, such as acorns and walnuts. Even tough, little hawthorn berries and sycamore wings are fruits. Fruits all have seeds protected inside a container. The container may be the soft flesh of a plum or the hard shell of a hazelnut. You can discover the seeds inside different fruits. Some examples are given here. If you want to try others, use fruits bought from your local grocery store since some wild berries are poisonous.

orange   apple

plum

lemon

apricot

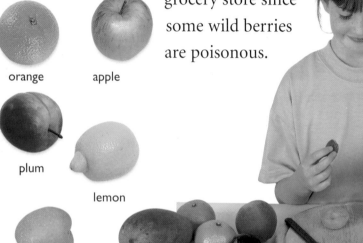

YOU WILL NEED

Looking at apple seeds: apple, chopping board, sharp knife, tweezers, magnifying glass.

Looking inside a nut: hazelnuts, nutcracker, scissors, magnifying glass.

How a seed grows: blotting paper or newspaper, glass jar, broad bean or runner bean seed, water.

Tropical seeds: avocado stone, three cocktail sticks, jar, water, gloves, pot, trowel, potting compost.

◄ **Center spot**

These fruits are soft, fleshy, and sweet. Like most fruits, they have grown from the reproductive ovaries inside female flowers. Open any fruit, and inside you will find seeds.

Looking at apple seeds

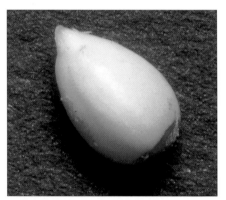

1 Cut open an apple with a sharp knife. Inside you will find several brown seeds in the middle. Use the tweezers to remove as many of the seeds as you want.

2 Use the tweezers to carefully remove the soft outer skin of a seed. Underneath the skin, you will find the slippery white seed. Treat it carefully—it is very delicate.

3 Look under a magnifier to see the embryo (at the tip). The rest of the seed is the cotyledon, which provides food so the embryo will grow into a new root and shoot.

Looking inside a nut

1 Nuts are fruits that have their seeds inside a hard shell. Carefully crack open a hazelnut with a pair of nutcrackers, and look for the nut kernel (seed) inside.

2 Use scissors to scrape off the dark outer skin from the kernel. You should then be able to separate the white hazelnut into two halves. Look at these with a magnifying glass.

3 Inside the nut is a tiny embryo. This part grows into roots and a stem. The two larger parts are the cotyledons, which supply energy for the sprouting seed to grow.

How a seed grows

1 Curl blotting paper inside a jar. Push a bean seed halfway down between the paper and the glass. Add water to a depth of ¾in and stand the jar in a light, warm place.

2 When the seed germinates, you will see the root growing downward. Turn the jar so that the root points to the right. What do you think will happen?

As the root continues to grow, it changes direction so that it is growing downward again.

Tropical seeds

1 An avocado stone is the seed of the avocado plant. Clean off any flesh left on the stone, and then carefully push three cocktail sticks into the stone, as shown above.

2 Fill a jar with water and suspend the stone, so that it just touches the waterline. Keep the jar in a warm, shady place, and top up the water regularly.

3 When roots begin to grow downward, plant the stone in a pot filled with compost. Place the pot where the air is warm and humid, and wait for your seedling to grow.

Life in the forest

People who live in forests build their homes from materials found in the forest. In South America, the Yanomami tribe's large, round huts are made with trees bent into a dome shape, lashed with vines and thatched with palm leaves. The Yanomami sleep on the roof in hammocks made of woven grasses, slung from the rafters. Scientists who work in rainforests sometimes build temporary shelters with branches. You can build a shelter by following these instructions, but you may need the help of an adult. When looking for branches to make your shelter with, take an adult with you. Collect the branches from your backyard or a public area. Do not cut them from trees—always gather them from the ground, where they have fallen naturally.

> ### YOU WILL NEED
> five sturdy branches, rope or thick string, a friend or adult to help, ropes or strings, eight pegs, tarpaulin, ground sheet, two poles.

▲ Temperate forests
Beech, ash, and oak grow in this northern European forest. Birds and squirrels live in the trees. Bluebells and wood anemones grow on the forest floor. Worms, moles, and badgers burrow underground. Larger animals include deer, wild pigs, and bears.

▲ Conifer forests
Hemlocks, cypresses, and giant redwoods grow in conifer forests in North America. Woodpeckers and chipmunks search for food in the trees. Ferns grow on the forest floor. Moose and beavers live near lakes, and black bears scavenge for food.

▲ Trees in the savanna
The African savanna is dotted with drought-resistant trees, such as baobabs (bottle trees) and acacias. Herds of zebra, antelope, and gazelles feed on grass. Taller giraffes and elephants can reach up into the trees for fresh leaves.

▲ Tropical rainforest
Many trees and climbing plants live in tropical rainforests, such as the Amazon of South America. Monkeys and brightly colored birds live high up in the trees, where there is light and food. Dense, rotting vegetation covers the ground.

Build a shelter

1 Lash the ends of two sturdy branches together with rope or string. Stand the branches upright to make an A-frame. You could tie the A-frame to a tree for extra support.

2 Lash two more branches together. Stand them upright about 6¼ft from the first A-frame. Place a lighter branch on top to make a ridge pole and lash it in place.

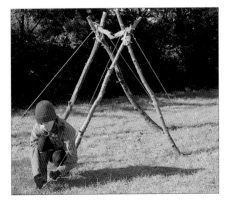

3 Attach two ropes or strings to each of the A-frames and peg the ropes securely into the ground. Now throw a tarpaulin over the ridge pole to form the roof.

4 Attach ropes or strings to the eyeholes in the corners of the tarpaulin, and peg them securely into the ground. Stretch the tarpaulin tight to make the roof.

5 Thread string through the eyeholes on opposite sides of the ground sheet, to make the sheet into a sort of tube. Push two poles inside the sheet, one on each side.

6 Pull the two poles apart to make a stretcher shape that will fit inside the shelter. This will form the hammock, so that you will be able to rest off the ground.

7 Wedge the stretcher inside your shelter, so that the poles rest on the outside of the upright A-frames. Make sure your hammock is secure and will not slip down the poles.

Now it's time to try out your hammock and take a well-earned break!

Soil erosion

All around the world, rainforests are being cut down at an alarming rate. At the beginning of the 1900s, tropical forests covered about twice the area they do today. Experts estimate that an area of rainforest about the size of England is lost each year. One of the main reasons for this is logging —the felling of trees for timber. Many rainforest trees are made of valuable hardwoods, such as teak and mahogany, which are used for building houses and making furniture. Trees are also cleared to create roads and new pasture for cattle.

The roots of trees and other plants help to hold forest soil together. When the trees are felled, the soil is left bare. During heavy rainfall, the earth is washed away, just as it is in the first project. However, when forests are left alone, they sustain themselves indefinitely, recycling water and nutrients from the soil. You can see how this works by growing a mini-jungle. The bottle or jar reproduces the warm, moist conditions and constant high temperatures of a rainforest. The plants recycle their own moisture, so they rarely need watering.

▲ **Vanishing forests**
This illustration shows the effects of deforestation. Tree roots help to hold the soil in place, and leaves absorb the force of falling rain. When forests are cut down, soil is washed away, and exposed earth dries up and hardens.

YOU WILL NEED

house plant, two plastic cups, plant pot, compost or soil mix, two watering cans.

Looking at soil erosion

1 Fit the house plant into the neck of one of the plastic cups. Fill the empty plant pot with compost or soil. Place the pot into the neck of the other plastic cup.

2 Pour water on to the house plant and into the pot of soil. What happens? You will find that water passes more quickly through the pot without the plant.

Water passing through the pot without the plant is muddy, because more soil has been washed through. Water passes more slowly through the pot with the plant. It will trickle through almost clear.

Plant a mini-jungle

1 Wash your large plastic bottle or jar to make sure that it is clean. Place handfuls of gravel into the bottom of the bottle, to make the lowest layer of the mini-jungle.

2 Mix a little charcoal with the compost or soil mix. Add a deep layer of compost mixture on top of the gravel, and then smooth out the soil so that it is level.

3 Make some large holes for the plants in the soil with a spoon or trowel. Then gently lift the plants out of their pots and lower them into the holes you have made.

4 Tamp the soil down around the base of each plant. You can use a spoon or a trowel to do this, if you find it difficult to reach that far with your fingers.

5 Spray the plants and soil quite thoroughly with water from a plant sprayer, or using a watering can with a sprinkler attachment. This is your tropical rain!

6 Put the lid on the bottle or jar, and your mini-jungle is complete. The water you have sprayed is recycled inside the bottle or jar, so you will not need to water your jungle often. Moisture from the plants condenses on the sides of the bottle or jar. It will then drip down into the soil, to be reused.

The balance of life

Life on Earth is a vast jigsaw of plant and animal activity. The world can be split into vegetation regions according to the kind of plants that thrive there. Scientists often break down the vegetation regions into smaller units, such as tropical rainforests or freshwater lakes. They might go further to identify individual trees or a pond. Each unit, where the creatures living there interact with each other, is called an ecosystem.

An ecosystem is a community of living things, or organisms, that all depend on each other. An aquarium like the one in the project is a miniature freshwater ecosystem. All plants need particular conditions of soil and climate to survive. Animals also survive by adapting to, and interacting with, their surroundings and the local climate.

If a particular species from an ecosystem is removed, the existence of other living things is threatened. If the plants on which a certain caterpillar feeds are destroyed, the caterpillars die. Eventually, the birds that feed on the caterpillars, and the foxes that feed on the birds would starve.

▲ Building an ecosystem

When there is enough warmth and moisture in an area of bare, rocky land, simple plants grow. The first to take hold are mosses and lichens. They are followed by tough grasses, which hold the soil together. As they die and rot, they add nutrients to the soil, preparing it for bigger plants to grow. Soon there is enough to support small shrubs and tough trees, such as pines, and eventually deciduous trees such as oaks. This process is called vegetation succession. It would take about 200 years for deciduous woodland to evolve from the moss and lichen stage.

Feeding habits ▶

Humans and animals depend on other living things for food. This picture shows how this food chain or web works. A grasshopper eats a leaf of grass, a thrush may eat the grasshopper, and a kestrel may eat the thrush. When the kestrel dies, bacteria break its body down and add nutrients to the soil, so that new plants can grow. Herbivorous animals eat plants only. Carnivores are meat eaters, and omnivores eat both animals and plants. Plants make their own food from sunlight, and so they are called autotrophs (self-feeders).

Make your own aquarium ecosystem

1 Put the gravel in a net. Rinse it in a plastic bowl of water, or run it under the cold water tap in the sink. This will discourage the formation of green algae.

2 Spread the gravel unevenly over base of the tank to a depth of about 1¼in. Add rocks and pieces of wood. These give surfaces for snails to feed on.

3 Fill the tank to about the halfway mark with tap water. Pour the water gently from a pitcher to avoid disturbing the landscape and churning up the gravel.

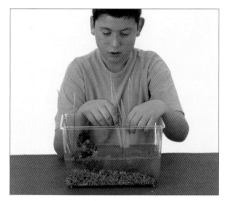

4 Add some water plants from an aquarium store. Keep some of them in their pots, but remove the others gently. Then root them in the gravel.

5 Now add a pitcherful of pondwater. This will contain organisms, such as *daphnia* (water fleas), which add to the life of your aquarium. You can buy pondwater in a garden store.

6 Add a few of the water animals you have collected from local ponds, such as tadpoles in frog spawn, or water snails. Take care not to overcrowd the aquarium.

7 Place the tank in bright light, but not in direct sunlight. You can watch the plants in the tank grow. Keep the water clean by removing dead matter off the gravel every few weeks.

Animal tracks and footprints

Wild creatures in the forest usually run away when humans approach. However, you can learn a lot about birds and other animals by looking at their tracks. You could go to a wood with an adult to hunt for animal tracks on soft or wet ground. The banks of streams and rivers are often criss-crossed by prints from animals who have gone there to drink.

Different groups of animals (mammals, birds, reptiles, and amphibians) leave different tracks. The first project shows you how to look for these prints. Tracks give clues about the size and weight of the animal. They also show how animals move —whether they run, hop, slide or slither. Large, heavy birds for example, such as geese, waddle along—shifting their weight from side to side. Their prints show that they place one foot in front of the other and slightly to the side, rather like the way humans walk. Small birds, such as sparrows and finches, hop along on thin legs and feet. They leave tracks of tiny prints running side by side. Draw the prints or take a photograph, and record in a notebook the date and place, ground conditions, and other observations. The second project shows you how to make casts of the most interesting footprints.

▲ Out and about

Study the tracks that you have found very carefully. What do they tell you about the way the animal that made them moved—did it hop, run, or waddle? Use a field guide to animal tracks to help you identify the animals that left them.

YOU WILL NEED

magnifying glass, camera, notebook,

pencil, field guide.

Animal tracks

1 When you find a footprint, count the number of toes. Can you see any claws? A fox's paw is rounded, with four toes and claws. Take photos or make drawings of animal tracks you see.

2 Deer have narrow, split hooves with just two toes. They leave deep tracks, because they walk with all their weight on their toes, rather than evenly spread throughout their feet.

3 Most birds have long, spindly feet, with either three or four toes. All ducks and some wading birds have webbed feet. The web shows up in the outline of the print.

Footprint cast

1 Find a clear animal track, either in sand or dry mud. Remove any loose twigs or leaves around the print. (Remember to wear gloves if you are working in soil.)

2 Look for bird footprints in wet sand or mud. Tracks show the size of the bird that made it, and what group of birds it belongs to. Use a field guide to identify the bird that made the print.

3 Bend a strip of card into a ring large enough to fit around the print, and fasten the card ring with a paper clip. Place the ring over the print.

4 Mix the plaster of Paris with a little water in a bowl, according to the instructions on the package. Stir the mixture until it is a thick and even paste with no lumps.

5 Carefully spoon enough plaster of Paris onto the print to cover it completely. After 15 minutes, the cast will be dry enough for you to pick it up.

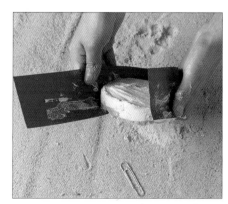

6 Use a trowel to prize the cast loose. Carefully peel off the paper ring. Clean up the cast by brushing off any loose soil or sand with a scrubbing brush.

7 Allow the plaster cast to dry for 24 hours. After this, you could paint or varnish the cast. Try painting the raised footprint one color and the background another color.

Finished casts of dog and bird footprints.

Searching for insects

Insects make up three-quarters of all animal species (kinds) on the Earth. Insects are everywhere, so they are easy to find. The best place to start is your backyard or a local park. If there is a good range of plants, up to 300 species of beetles can be found in a very small area, such as gardens. There may be up to 200 kinds of flies, 90 different bugs and many species of bees, ants, wasps, moths and butterflies.

▲ **Feet tasters**
The housefly has taste sensors on its feet. It sucks up its liquid through spongy mouthparts as soon as it lands.

To identify the species living in a particular area, scientists mark a square, and search all the places where creatures hide —under leaves, stones, and logs, and in tiny crevices in trees. Scientists may leave pitfall traps in the ground, or hang traps in the trees. You can find creatures locally using the type of trap demonstrated in the first project. The second project shows you how to make a simple pooter, that enables you to collect insects without harming them. Wear gloves when handling insects, because some may sting or bite. Always take an adult out with you.

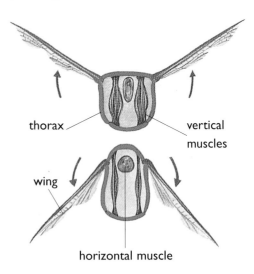

▲ **How insects fly**
Insects have no muscles in their wings. Instead the wings are hinged to the insect's thorax. They move up and down as the thorax changes shape. As the roof of the thorax is pulled down, the wings flick up. As the ends of the thorax are pulled in, the wings flick down.

Pitfall trap

1 If you have a backyard, ask an adult to show you a place where you can dig a small hole. Use a trowel to dig a hole in damp earth, which is large enough for the jar to fit in.

2 Place the jar in the hole. Firm the earth back around the sides of the jar with your hands. Put small, fresh leaves in the bottom of the jar for minibeast bait.

3 Place some small stones around the trap, and balance a large flat stone or tile on top, to prevent the minibeast trap from filling up with rain. Leave it overnight.

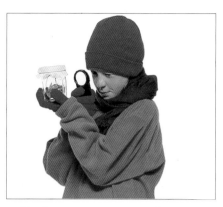

4 In the morning, remove the jar. Place a piece of muslin over the top and secure it with a rubber band. Study any minibeasts you have caught using a magnifying glass.

5 Use a field guide to identify the minibeasts you have caught. When you have finished, remember to release the creatures near to where you found them.

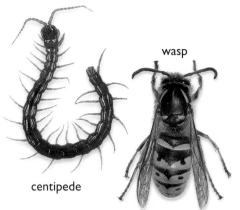

wasp

centipede

▲ **Show a leg**

Centipedes, like insects, are members of the arthropod group. They have many legs, one pair on each body segment. Adult insects, such as this queen wasp, have bodies in three main sections and six legs. Most also have wings.

Make a pooter

YOU WILL NEED

Pitfall trap: garden gloves, trowel, glass jar, fresh leaves, small stones, large flat stone or tile, muslin, rubber band, magnifying glass, field guide.

Make a pooter: small plastic bottle, scissors, nonhardening modeling material, wide bendable straws, small piece of muslin, rubber band, sharp pencil.

1 Cut off the bottom of the plastic bottle. Roll out one large and one small ball of modeling material. Flatten out the large ball and mould it over the bottom of the bottle.

2 To make a filter, cut a short piece of straw. Secure a piece of muslin around the straw with a rubber band. Push the other end through the small lump of modeling material.

3 Fit the filter into the neck of the bottle by molding the modeling material. Make a hole in the bottom flap with a sharp pencil. Push a long straw into the hole you have made.

4 Look for a small insect to study. (Big insects would get damaged.) Aim the end of the long straw over the insect. Suck on the short straw to draw the insect safely into the pooter.

5 When you have finished studying your insect, take it back to where you found it. To release the insect, carefully remove the bottom flap and shake the insect out.

What is an insect?

Birds, reptiles, and mammals all have internal skeletons to provide a framework for their bodies. Insects are different—they have skeletons on the outside. Their soft body parts are protected by a hard case called an exoskeleton. This forms a waterproof barrier around the insect. It prevents the insect from drying out and air from passing through. Unlike birds and mammals, insects are cold-blooded animals. This means the temperature of an insect's body is about the same as its surroundings. To warm up, an insect basks in the sunshine. When it gets too hot, it moves into the shade.

Insects are fragile. It can be difficult to pick them up and examine them without harming them. When studying insects, use a notebook to record what you see. Write down the date, time, weather conditions, and place where you found the insect. Use a field guide to help you make an identification. The projects here show you how to keep a record of the insects that you see. Look at the mouthparts and antennae. Think about the shape of the insect's body. Is it short or long? Does the insect have hard wing cases, or long legs?

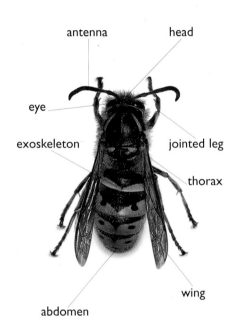

antenna · head · eye · exoskeleton · jointed leg · thorax · wing · abdomen

▲ Wasp sections

The bodies of adult insects have three sections—head, thorax, and abdomen. Like this wasp, each section is made of small plates that fit together at flexible joints. The head carries the mouth parts, antennae, and eyes. The legs and wings are attached to the thorax. The abdomen contains the reproductive organs and part of the digestive system.

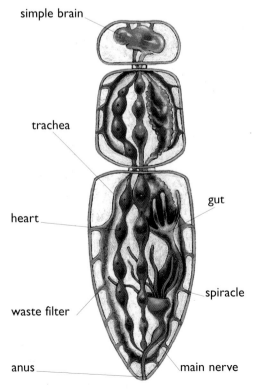

simple brain · trachea · heart · waste filter · anus · gut · spiracle · main nerve

◀ Inside the insect

An insect's internal systems are protected by its hard exoskeleton. This diagram shows the main systems separated and colored to make them clear. The nervous system (purple) sends messages from the senses to the brain. In the respiratory system (gray), air enters the body through tiny holes along each side of the insect's body, called spiracles. Pipes called tracheae carry the air to other parts of the body. In the circulatory system (red), several hearts, arranged in a row, pump blood around the body. The digestive system (green, orange) processes food.

Drawing insects

1 Find an insect and use the magnifying glass to study it closely. Start by drawing three ovals to show the head, the thorax, and the abdomen of the insect.

2 Can you see the insect's legs? Copy them on your drawing. Now copy the size and shape of the insect's antennae. Draw the eyes and add the outline of the wings.

3 Now draw any markings that you notice on the insect's body and wings (if it has them). Finish your drawing by coloring it in as accurately as you can.

Insect survey

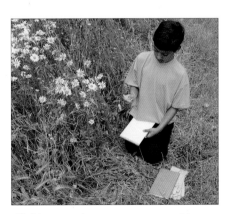

1 Find an area of long grass. Wearing gloves to protect your hands, use the tent pegs, a measuring tape, and string to mark a square measuring 1 yard on each side.

2 What insects can you find inside the square? Use a collecting jar and a magnifying glass to study them. Write down what you have found in a notebook.

3 Now mark out a square yard in a different place. Try an area with flowers or a hedge. You may find aphids and ladybirds on plant stems, and shieldbugs under leaves.

4 Move a fallen log to see what kinds of insects live underneath. Make sure you wear gloves to protect your hands. You may find beetles under logs, and woodlice and earwigs under bark.

5 Still wearing gloves, carefully look under some stones. What kinds of creatures prefer this dark, damp habitat? You may find worms, snails, ground beetles, or an ants' nest.

Use your field guide to identify your discoveries. How many different species did you find in each area? Make a chart to record the results of your survey.

Studying insect life

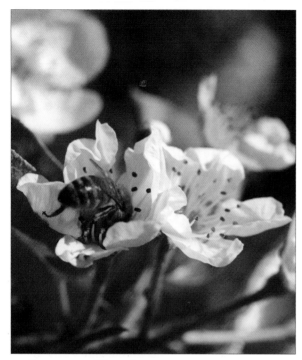

▲ Insect pollination

This wasp is visiting a flower to feed on its sugary nectar. It sucks up the nectar with its tongue, to feed the larvae (young) in its nest. As the wasp reaches into the center of the flower, pollen from the flower rubs off on the insect's body. This is then carried by the wasp to next flower.

Woods are great places to go insect watching. Trees offer food and shelter from the weather, so they are an ideal habitat for insects. The number of insects you find may depend on the season. In the spring, wild flowers bloom and attract insects. In the summer, the woods offer insects sunny clearings and cool shade. Choose a large tree and make a survey of all the insects you can find on a single branch. Make a tree trap to catch insects active at night.

Many insects depend on plants, but many plants depend on insects too. Insects help to pollinate plants by carrying pollen from the same plant to another of its species. Many plants have pink, red or orange flowers, because these are the colors that butterflies see well. Other flowers have special markings called nectar guides, leading from the base of the petals. Some show up only in ultraviolet light. Insects such as bees have eyes that are sensitive to this light, and they follow these guides to the middle of the flower.

Human vision

Insect vision

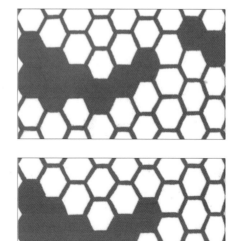

◀ Seeing is believing

Insect vision is very different from ours. Experts think each lens of an insect's compound eye sees a small part of a scene. This gives a mosaiclike view that is built up into a bigger picture. These diagrams compare how we see a moving insect, and what experts think an insect sees. An insect can sense tiny movements our eyes would hardly notice, because they have many more lenses that are affected.

4 Put some damp kitchen paper in a corner of the box to provide moisture. Carefully transfer your caterpillars from the collecting jar to the box. Cover with the lid.

5 Check your caterpillars every day, and replace the damp kitchen paper. Record how much they eat and how big they are. Remember to replace the leaves daily.

6 Watch how your caterpillars feed and move around on the leaves. Record the dates when you see them molting (shedding skin). How many times did they shed their skins?

7 When it has finished growing, the caterpillar will change into a pupa, or chrysalis. It will attach itself to the stem of a food plant, and form a new skin. Make a note of the date.

8 Check your pupa every day, and write down the date when you see the case splitting. Compare your two dates. How long did the insect spend as a pupa?

9 You will see a butterfly or moth struggle out of the old skin. The insect rests and pumps blood into its crumpled wings to straighten them out before flying off.

June-July	caterpillar feeds	
end July		pupa forms
mid-August		butterfly emerges

Keep a chart of the life cycles of your insects.

When the caterpillars become adult moths or butterflies, it is time to let them go. Take the insects back to where you found them. Lift the lid off the box, and let them fly away.

Crawling colonies

Unlike most insects, ants live in colonies. They are known as social insects, as opposed to solitary insects. Ants are different to flying insects, such as butterflies and bees, yet they behave in a similar way. An ant colony is like an underground city with millions of insects, each with its own role to play. Queen ants (of which there may be several in one nest) lay eggs. Undeveloped females called workers perform the essential tasks of the colony. They scurry around, searching for food, and bring it to the nest.

The key to the smooth running of the colony is good communication. Ants cannot see well, so they communicate by touch and smell. When two ants meet, they touch antennae (feelers). When an ant finds a food source, it hurries back to the nest, pressing its body close to the ground as it runs. This leaves a trail of scent, which the other ants can follow to reach the food.

eggs   queen's chamber   rubbish

pupae

workers   young ants hatch   worker and larvae

▲ Inside an ants' nest

Ants' nests are usually underground. A nest has many chambers, or rooms, and passages. Different chambers contain the eggs, larvae (young), pupae, and the queen. Other chambers are used to store food and trash. Worker ants alter the temperature of the nest by opening or closing passages.

YOU WILL NEED

garden gloves, peeled ripe fruit,

piece of paper, magnifying glass.

Watching ant trails

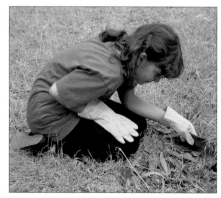

1 Wearing gloves, find a trail of ants. Follow the trail to discover where the ants are going. Does the trail lead to food? Rub out part of the trail and see what happens.

2 Now put fruit down on a piece of paper near the trail of ants. The paper will make it easier to see the ants. When the workers find the fruit, watch and see what happens.

3 Once an ant has laid a scent trail to the fruit, others will follow. Move the fruit to another part of the paper. What happens next? Do the ants go straight to the new food site?

Make an ant home

YOU WILL NEED

ruler, scissors, dark-colored paper, large jar, tape, garden gloves, trowel, earth, fallen leaves, paintbrush, jar containing ants, ripe fruit or jelly, kitchen paper, muslin.

1 Measure and cut a piece of dark-colored paper that is large enough to fit around the jar. Secure the paper in position around the jar with tape.

2 Wearing a pair of gloves, use the trowel to fill the jar with earth until the jar is almost full. Carefully place a few leaves on top of the earth.

3 Capture some garden ants using a paintbrush and collecting jar. Let the ants crawl on to the paintbrush. Then tap the jar, so that the ants fall in. Transfer the ants to their new home.

4 Feed your ants with a piece of ripe fruit or jelly. Some damp kitchen paper will provide moisture. Feed your ants daily and refresh the leaves and moist paper regularly.

5 Cover the top of the jar with a piece of muslin, so that the ants cannot escape. Secure the muslin with tape. Keep your ant home in a cool place.

6 After a few days, remove the tape and lift the paper to observe your ant home. There will now be winding tunnels, built by the ants, against the sides of the jar.

If you have caught a queen ant, you may see the workers tending the eggs or larvae in special chambers.

Discovering birds

There are birds living in all areas of the world. They inhabit icy polar regions, tropical wet rainforests, and scorching hot deserts. Birds are also found in crowded cities, on high mountains, and remote islands.

Birds vary in size. The tiny hummingbird of Cuba is no larger than a bumblebee. The African ostrich, at the other extreme, stands 8 foot high. Birds are warm-blooded creatures like mammals, but they lay eggs, as reptiles and amphibians do. Unlike other animals, birds' bodies are covered with strong, lightweight feathers. These help birds to fly, although there are a few species that cannot fly.

There are more than 8,600 different species (kinds) of birds. Scientist divide all these birds into groups called orders. The 28 bird orders are divided into smaller groups, called families, and each family contains several species. Species in the same family tend to have a similar body shape, which makes them suited to a certain way of life. For example, ducks have wide bodies and webbed feet to help them move through water.

The largest bird species often live the longest. Giant albatrosses can live for 80 years. Small songbird species, such as blue tits and sparrows, may live for just one year.

skull
nostril
neck
backbone
keel
wingbone
ribcage
ankle
toe

▲ Body shape

Birds have a basic body shape that varies in size and color according to species. All birds have a beak, instead of jaws with teeth, and scaly legs and feet. Flying birds have a skeleton that is geared for efficient flight. Powerful wings and a feathered tail help with stability and steering. The wings and legs are arranged close to the center of the body, to help with balance.

left eye socket

right eye socket

▲ Field of vision for a woodcock

A woodcock eats earthworms and insects. It does not need to spot prey like an owl does but must look for enemies. Its eyes are on the side of its head. This enables it to see all around itself.

YOU WILL NEED

Looking at diving birds: field guide, stopwatch or watch with a second hand, notebook, pen, drawing pad, colored pencils.
Drawing birds: drawing pad, pen and pencils, notebook.

Looking at diving birds

1 Choose a pond or a lake for bird-watching. See where different species feed. Notice where they dive and reappear. Use a field guide to help you to identify species.

2 Now find out how long the different birds spend under the water. Use your stopwatch to time their dives. Do they feed underwater, or bring food to the surface?

3 Record the times in your notebook. Which bird stays underwater for the longest time? Do you think that this is affected by the depth of the water?

4 In your notebook, make a rough map of the pond or lake. When you get home, do a neater version and color it in. Show vegetation such as grass or reeds.

5 On your map, use different colored pencils to mark where various species of birds swim and feed. Remember to draw a key to explain which bird each color represents.

Drawing birds

1 You do not have to be a great artist to draw birds. Study the shape of the bird. Notice how long the neck is. Start with simple ovals for the head and body.

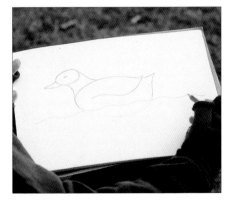

2 Look at the shape of the bird's beak, and at its neck and tail. If you can see the legs, how long are they? Can you see the feet? Add these details to your drawing.

3 Now add a pair of wings and other details, such as the face and tail. Make notes about the bird's coloring. so that you can color your drawing in later.

Bird-watching

Birds are among the easiest animals to spot and study from your home or school. To see a wider range of species (kinds), you could try bird-watching in a local park, pond, or woodland area. Always take an adult with you. Birds are shy creatures with sharp eyesight and hearing. They are always on the lookout for enemies, so keep very quiet and still when bird-watching. If you make yourself a hide, like the one shown, bird-watching will be much easier.

Using binoculars

1 Lightweight binoculars are very useful on bird-watching trips. Remove them from the case, and hang them around your neck so you are ready to use them.

2 When you see a bird, do not look down, or you may lose sight of it. Keep watching it, and slowly raise the binoculars to your eyes. Try to avoid sudden movements.

3 Now adjust the focusing wheel on your binoculars, to bring the bird into focus. You may find this difficult to do at first, but it will become easier with practice.

Build a hide

1 You will need a friend to help you. Lay four short canes on the ground in a square. Tie the ends with string. Make another square the same size, to form the roof.

2 Get your friend to stand inside the base. Your friend should hold the roof in position, while you tie four long canes to the base and roof to form the sides.

3 Now strengthen the structure of your hide. Add two long canes to make cross-pieces on opposite sides of the hide. Tie the canes in place with a piece of string.

4 Drape your hide with the canvas or tarpaulin. Add a smaller piece for the roof. Fasten the edges with safety pins. For extra security, fix the base to the ground with tent pegs.

5 Now cover the cloth with some leaves and twigs. These will camouflage your hide, so that it will blend in with the woods and will be less obvious to birds.

6 Once inside the hide, look out through the gaps in the seams, between the safety pins. Try using your binoculars. Keep still and quiet, and birds will soon approach.

A tipi is another, simpler kind of hide. You will need four to six canes, string, a tarpaulin, safety pins and maybe tent pegs. Fan the canes to form a pyramid shape, and tie the top ends with string. Drape the tarpaulin over this, and fasten it with safety pins.

Camouflage the tipi with leaves and twigs. Leave a gap to look through the cover with your binoculars.

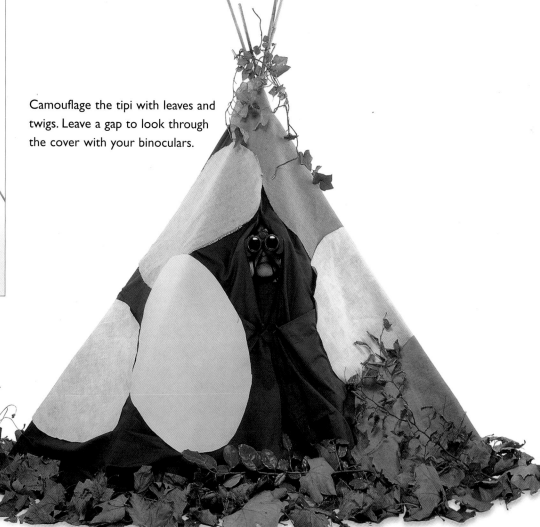

Listening to birds

The voices of singing birds that seem beautiful to us often have many meanings. A bird's song identifies what species (kind) it is as well as each bird as an individual. Male birds sing to establish their own territories. A territory is a patch of ground where the birds intend to breed and feed. In Antarctica, a parent penguin finds its chick among thousands of other chicks by its cry. Birds also call to warn of danger and to attract a mate. Birds that flock together use contact calls to keep in a tight group.

You can make a birdbath for the birds who visit your garden in the first project. Listening to birdsong is a good way of identifying birds. The best times of the day to listen to birds are at dawn and dusk, when they sing the loudest. It is fun to make recordings of the different bird songs that you come across. Use a portable tape recorder with a long cord, so that you can position the microphone farther away. Tape the microphone to a stick, so that the sounds of your hands will not be recorded. Headphones will let you check what you are recording. To achieve even better results, make yourself a sound reflector, as shown in the third project.

▲ Hooters of the night

An owl's night-time hooting is a well-recognized sound. Owls have excellent eyesight. This makes them good hunters in the dark. Some have flat disk-shaped faces. These help direct sound into the ears at the side of the head.

YOU WILL NEED

trowel, rubber gloves, large dish or old trash can lid, stones, bucket of water.

Build a birdbath

1 Use your trowel to dig a hollow in the earth. It should be big enough to fit your trash can lid or dish. Place the dish in the hollow, and press it down firmly, making sure it is flat.

2 Now place a few large stones in your trash can lid or dish. Birds who come to your garden will use these stones to stand on, to get in and out of your birdbath.

3 Pour water into the bath, to a depth of about 4-6in. The tops of the stones should stick up above the water, so that birds can spot them and land on them easily.

Taping birdsong

1 Become familiar with the songs of birds that live in your area by listening to recordings on CD or cassette tape. You can borrow these from your local library.

2 Outside, position yourself behind a tree or bush, if possible. Set up the microphone on a long cord by a bird table, or near a perch where you see a bird singing.

3 To record, press the record and pause buttons, releasing the pause button when you want to record. Listen with the headphones, and note down the time, place, and weather.

When you get home, listen to the calls you have recorded very carefully. Most field guides give details of birdcalls and will be able to help you identify the songs.

Sound reflector

1 Cover the inside of an old umbrella with sheets of foil. Carefully bend the foil over the edges of the umbrella and tape it down securely with tape. Overlap the sheets of foil as needed.

2 Fix the mike to the stem of the umbrella, with the mike head pointing toward the shade. Try the mike in different positions—about 6-8in away from the shade.

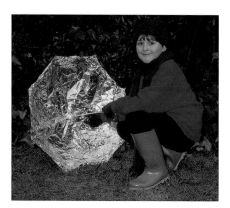

3 Set up your reflector where birds are singing. The reflector will channel sounds and amplify them (make them louder). Give birds time to get to used to this strange object.

Birds' nests

Nests are warm, safe places where birds lay eggs, and where the nestlings (baby birds) develop after they have hatched. Birds do not sleep in their nests at night. Instead, they roost on perches in sheltered places, such as hedges and trees.

Constructing the nest is usually the female's job. The first step is to choose a good site. Then the materials are gathered. Twigs, leaves, feathers, moss, wool, and mud are all used by various birds. The nest-building bird pushes the materials into place, and hollows out the inside with her body. The finished nest may be lined with soft materials, such as feathers, to protect the eggs.

Nesting birds are fascinating to study. Attract birds into your garden, and help them to nest and raise their young by building a nesting box in the early spring. You may see birds fly by with nesting materials in their beaks, looking for a place to build. Many birds build their nests wedged in the forks of tree branches. Nest-building uses up a lot of time and energy. It may take between a week and a month, yet most nests last for just one breeding season, and are ruined by winter weather.

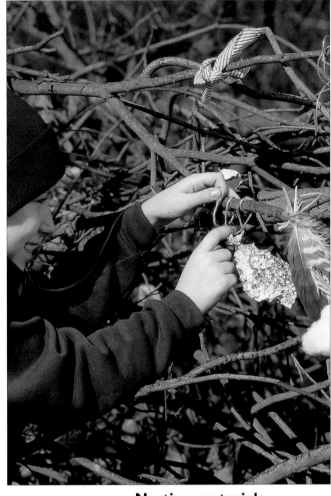

▲ Nesting materials

In the spring, try hanging nesting material from branches or a window sill. You can use wool, string, grass, moss and feathers. You could also try paper tissue, straw, and animal hair. Different bird species like different materials. Try and find out which materials are chosen by various birds.

Template for nesting box

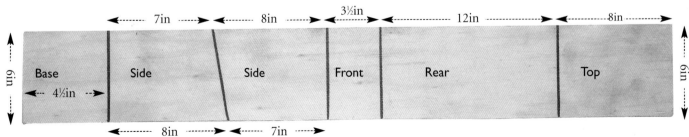

	7in	8in	3½in	12in	8in

6in | Base 4½in | Side | Side | Front | Rear | Top | 6in

8in | 7in

Use ⅝in thick pine or plywood. Ask an adult to cut pieces to the sizes and shapes shown above.

Finding out about feathers

I Study a bird's flight feather under a magnifying glass. Split the feather's barbs (individual strands). You can now observe the barbules (the fringed edges).

2 Repair the feather's surface, just as a bird does during preening. Smooth the barbs between your finger and thumb, so that they join back together properly.

3 Now try another experiment. Add a little water to some paint, and brush it on your flight feather. What happens to the paint? Why do you think this is?

Dissect an owl pellet

YOU WILL NEED

Finding out about feathers:

feathers, magnifying glass, water, paint, water pot, paintbrush.

Dissect an owl pellet: rubber gloves, owl pellet, bowl, warm water, dishwashing detergent, tweezers, paper towel, small box, tissue paper.

I Wear rubber gloves for this project. First, soak the owl pellet in a bowl of warm water with a little dishwashing detergent added. Leave the pellet until it has softened.

2 Using a pair of tweezers, gently begin to pull the pellet apart. Inside, you will find the fur, teeth, skulls, and other bones of small animals that the owl has eaten.

3 Use the tweezers to carefully separate the bones from the fur. Wash the bones in warm, soapy water, and pat them dry gently with a paper towel.

Line a small box with tissue paper. Choose a bright color that will make the bones show up. Now arrange your bones. Can you identify the animal remains that you have found? There may be remains of voles, including skulls, jawbones, and leg bones. It can also contain small stones that the owl had swallowed to help with digestion.

Bird travel and flight

Many birds travel vast distances each year. They may travel to escape the chill of winter, to find food or a safe nesting site. Departure is often triggered by the shortening daylight hours of the fall. In the spring, the birds travel back again. These journeys are called migrations. Many species (kinds) do not feed while they travel, so must fatten up before they leave. Migrating birds face many dangers. They may get lost in storms or be killed by predators. Thousands die of hunger, thirst, and exhaustion.

Flying takes up a lot of energy, but has many advantages for birds. Hovering uses the most energy of all. However, birds are able to save their energy by gliding on air currents. Large birds soar upward into air currents, with their wings outstretched to trap as much air as possible. Making your own airfoil in the project opposite shows you how the shape of a wing produces lift. Then build a spiral model to see how birds circle in warm air currents without flapping their wings.

▲ Lift and flight

A bird's wing is slightly curved at the top, and flatter underneath. A shape like this, which is designed to provide uplift in flight, is called an airfoil. As the bird moves through the air, the curved shape makes the air travel faster over the wing than beneath it. This makes an area of low air pressure above the wing, which allows the bird to rise. Aircraft are able to fly, because their wings are a similar shape to a bird's wings.

Migration routes

● White storks travel from Europe to South Africa via Gibraltar or the Middle East.

● Short-tailed shearwaters fly the length of the Pacific ocean, from Alaska to the Tasman Sea.

● Arctic tern

● Peregrine falcons migrate from Canada to Argentina. They are also found in Europe and Asia.

● American golden plover

● Swallows migrate from northern Europe and Asia, to South Africa and back again—nearly 12,500 miles.

How a wing works

1 Cut a strip of paper about 12in long. Glue the ends together firmly. When the glue is dry, bend the paper into a wing shape, curved on top and flat underneath.

2 Mark the center of the wing. Thread a long piece of thread on to a needle and push it through the center of the wing. Gently pull the airfoil down the thread.

3 Now get a friend to hold the thread taut. Blow hard against the curved edge of the airfoil, and watch the wing rise up the thread—just as an airplane or a bird's wing lifts.

Soaring spiral

YOU WILL NEED

How a wing works: paper, scissors, glue, pencil, needle, thread.

Soaring spiral: thick paper, compass, pencil, colored pencils/felt-tipped pens, scissors, pencil with eraser on end, reel of thread, pin, thimble.

1 Use a compass and a pencil to draw a circle on a piece of paper. Now draw and color in a spiral shape with buzzards (or other birds) flying around it.

2 Carefully cut out the decorated paper spiral. Use a pencil to make the hole left in the center of the spiral by your compass, big enough to fit over the thimble.

3 Fit the pencil point into the reel. Put the pin in the eraser. Push the thimble through the hole in the paper spiral, so that it sits over the thimble. Balance the thimble on the pin.

4 Stand your model on a radiator. Now watch the buzzards circling around in the warm air currents that rise from the radiator. Your model must be well-balanced to work properly.

Physical and Material Marvels

We live in a world of engineering marvels—of soaring sky scrapers, wide-spanning bridges, and massive dams. We can communicate with almost everyone, anywhere on the Earth, and even in Space. This section shows the part that science and technology have played in setting the pace of change. Science accumulates knowledge about the world by observation, study, and experiment. Technology puts the knowledge into practical use as inventions, to improve the quality of life.

Chemical change

Over the past 100 years, scientists have invented many substances, such as plastics, medicines, and detergents, that we take for granted today. These substances are created by chemical reactions. In a chemical reaction, a new substance (called a product) is made as a result of other substances (called reactants) undergoing chemical change. Many chemical reactions happen naturally, such as oil (petrol) and gas, which form from the remains of animals and plants. They are called hydrocarbons, because they are mixtures of hydrogen and carbon.

The following experiments demonstrate the three main ways in which chemical reactions can happen—by passing electricity through substances, by heating them, or simply by mixing them together. In the first, electricity breaks down salty water to make chlorine (the disinfectant often used in swimming pools). In the second, heat turns sugar, which is made from carbon, hydrogen, and oxygen, into pure carbon. Finally, you make the gas used in some fire extinguishers by mixing bicarbonate of soda and vinegar together.

▲ **Checking up**
A technician is ensuring all the bottles of chemicals are correctly labeled. Accuracy is very important in science.

YOU WILL NEED
Electrolysis: battery (4–6 volts), bulb and holder, wires, wire strippers, screwdriver, paper clips, salt, jar, water.
Heat changes: old pan, teaspoon, sugar, stove.
Getting a reaction: teaspoon, bicarbonate of soda, glass bowl, vinegar, matches.

WARNING!

Please take care when using electrical equipment. Always have an adult present.

How oil is formed

The story of oil begins in warm seas full of living things. As they die, they fall to the bottom of the sea floor to decay into thick, black mud.

In time, mud is buried beneath many layers of sand, with clay in between. The sediments (deposits) sink deeper and deeper, and also become hotter.

After millions of years, the sediments fold under pressure. Oil from the black mud is forced into sandstones and trapped under the layers of clay.

Electrolysis

1 Connect the battery and bulb holder with wires, as shown here. Remove ½in of insulation from each end of wire. Use the paper clips to attach the wires to the battery.

2 Stir salt into a jar of water until no more dissolves. Dip the two bare wire ends into the mixture and hold them about ½in apart. Look for bubbles forming around them.

3 The bulb should light to show that electricity is passing through. Carefully sniff the jar from 8in away. What does it smell like? The smell is like swimming pools!

Heat changes

1 Make sure the pan is completely dry. Spread one teaspoonful of sugar across the bottom of the pan. Aim for a thin layer—about ¼in thick.

2 Place the pan on the stove and set to low heat. After a few minutes, the sugar will start to melt into a thick, brown liquid. You may begin to see a few wisps of steam.

3 The sugar starts to bubble as it breaks down and gives off steam. If you continue heating the sugar, the brown, sticky liquid will change to solid black carbon.

Getting a reaction

The gas is called carbon dioxide. Ask an adult to lower a lighted match into the bowl. The flame goes out when it meets the gas.

1 Place three heaped spoonfuls of bicarbonate of soda in the bowl. Cooks often add this white powder to vegetables, such as peas and carrots. It helps to keep their natural colour.

2 Carefully pour vinegar into the bowl. As the liquid mixes with the bicarbonate of soda, a chemical reaction happens. The mixture bubbles as a gas is given off.

Tests with yeast

For thousands of years, people all over the world have used yeast for brewing beer and baking bread. Yeast is a type of fungus that lives on the skins of many fruits. Just a spoonful of yeast contains millions of separate, single-celled (very simple) organisms. Each one works like a tiny chemical factory, taking in sugar, and giving out alcohol and carbon dioxide gas. While they feed, the yeast cells grow larger and then reproduce by splitting in half.

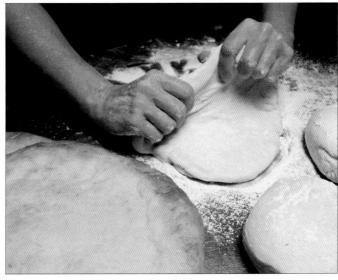

▲ Kneading dough
Bread is kneaded into a soft dough and then left in a warm place to rise. The dough is then kneaded again before it is baked. This process makes the yeast produce as many bubbles of gas as possible, so that the bread is light.

Yeast turns grape juice into alcoholic wine, and makes beer from mixtures of grain and water. When it is added to uncooked dough, yeast produces gas bubbles that make the bread light and soft. Brewing and baking are important modern industries that depend on yeast working quickly.

This project consists of four separate experiments. By comparing the results, you can discover the best conditions for yeast to grow. It needs a moist environment to be active. Lack of moisture makes the cells dry out and hibernate (sleep). Add water to dried, powdered yeast, and—even after many years—it will become active again.

Finding the best conditions

YOU WILL NEED

measuring cup, water, kettle, adhesive colored labels, four small glass jars, teaspoon, dried yeast granules, sugar, scissors, plastic wrap, three rubber bands, two heatproof bowls, ice cubes.

1 Half fill a kettle with water. Ask an adult to boil it for you, and then put it aside to cool. Boiling the water kills all living organisms that might stop the yeast from growing.

2 Label the glass jars, one to four. Put a level teaspoonful of dried yeast into each jar as shown here. Then put the same amount of sugar into each jar.

3 Pour ⅔cup of the cooled, boiled water into the first three jars. Stir the mixture to dissolve the sugar. Do not pour water into the fourth jar. Put this jar away in a warm place.

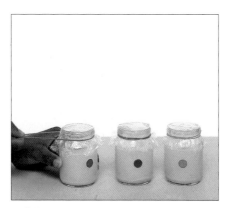

4 Cut out pieces of plastic wrap about twice a jar's width. Stretch one across the neck of each remaining jar, and secure it with a rubber band. Put the first jar in a warm place.

5 Place the second jar in a glass bowl. Put some ice cubes and cold water into the bowl. This will keep the jar's temperature close to freezing.

6 Place the third jar in another glass bowl. Pour in some hot water that is almost too hot to touch. Be careful not to use boiling water, or the jar may crack.

high temperature

warm temperature

7 Regularly check all four jars over the next two hours. As the ice around the second jar melts, add more to keep the temperature low. Add more hot water to keep the third jar hot.

cold temperature

dry jar

In the jar that was kept hot, the yeast is a cloudy layer at the bottom, killed by the heat. The jar that was kept cold has only a little froth on the surface, because the cold has slowed down the yeast.

The yeast that was kept warm has fed on the water and sugar, and its gas is pushing up the plastic wrap. In the dry jar, there are no signs of activity, because the yeast is hibernating.

Preservation and decay

Decay is the breaking up of dead organic matter, such as animals and plants. It results when invisible creatures called bacteria, and tiny fungi called molds, breed. The bodies of living plants and animals fight these agents of destruction, but as soon as the animals die, decay begins. Bacteria and molds that cause decay need water to live, so decay happens best in damp conditions.

▲ **Protected by the gods**
Turning the body of a great Egyptian pharaoh into a mummy was a complicated process. In addition to the preserving process, a jackal-masked priest performed sacred rituals.

The process of preserving something aims to stop it from decaying. The ancient Egyptians were skilled at mummifying (preserving) their kings' bodies. They removed moist internal organs, such as the intestines, heart, liver, and brain. Then they buried the body in natron, a kind of salt. This dried out all the fluids that speed up decay. The body was then wrapped in bandages. The bandages had been soaked in oily resins that killed bacteria and moulds in a similar way to modern antiseptic creams. You can practice slowing down and speeding up the process of decay in these two experiments.

What decays?

peeled carrot

unpeeled carrot

stone

plastic

unpeeled apple   peeled apple

wood

1 Peel one of the apples and one of the carrots. Line the tray with some newspaper. Add a layer of compost and place all the items on top. Add more compost to cover the items.

2 Dig a shallow hole in a shady spot and put the tray in it. Cover it with soil so that you can just see its top edges. Buried like this, the items will stay damp. Dig the tray up after a week.

Examine the results. Fruit and vegetables are attacked quickly by bacteria and molds, especially if they have no skins. Wood takes months to decay. Stone and plastic do not decay.

Tunnel in a landscape

1 Tear off about four long strips of masking tape. Curve the 18½ x 10½in rectangle of cardboard lengthways. Use the tape to hold the curve in place as shown above.

2 Copy the two templates A on to two 14½ x 12in pieces of thick card. Cut out the shapes. Attach each one to the sides of the tunnel, and secure with tape as shown above.

3 Fold the 17¾ x 16in thin card in half. Copy the arch template B onto the card. Cut out to make the two tunnel entrances. Stick these to the tunnel with masking tape as shown.

4 Scrunch newspaper into balls, and tape to the tunnel and landscape. Mix the flour and water to make a thick paste. Dip newspaper strips in the paste. Lay them over the tunnel.

5 Leave to dry overnight. When completely dry and hard, paint the tunnel and landscape green. Apply up to three coats, letting each one dry before you apply the next.

6 Paint the thin card to look like brick. Draw and cut out templates C and D. Draw around them onto the brick card, to make the keystone and lots of bricks. Allow paint to dry.

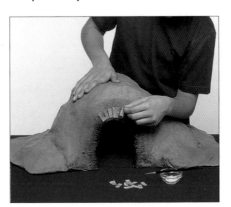

7 Glue the keystone at the top of the tunnel entrance. Then glue bricks around the arch at either side of the keystone. In real tunnels, there are keystones along the tunnel length.

8 Dip pieces of old sponge into green acrylic paint to make bushes. Leave to dry. Stick them on the landscape. Apply three coats of paint to the whole landscape.

The strength of a pyramid

Over a period of more than 4,500 years, people in different parts of the world built huge pyramids. The oldest Egyptian pyramids were started almost 4,600 years ago, while the youngest pyramids in Central America were finished about 600 years ago. Each one took a long time to build, sometimes over 50 years, and involved thousands of people.

Why did these civilizations opt for a pyramidal structure rather than a cube or a rectangle for their monuments? These experiments will help you to find out. In the first, by changing a cube into a pyramid, you end up with a structure that is three times taller than the original cube. A pyramid makes good use of material, by making the structure as high as possible. The second project shows that triangular shapes are more rigid than squares and do not collapse as easily. When an earthquake destroyed the Egyptian city of Cairo 700 years ago, the pyramids stood firm. Modern materials and technology make it possible to build tall, rectangular buildings that are strong and stable.

▲ Steep challenge

The Egyptians had no cranes to help them move the enormous slabs of stone used to build the pyramids. Workers built ramps of hard-packed earth. They hauled the slabs up these using plant-fiber ropes and wooden rollers. As the pyramid grew, the ramps became longer and steeper. When the pyramid was finished, the ramps were removed.

Bases and heights

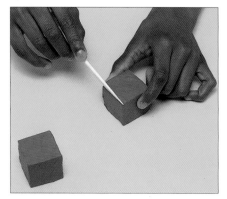

1 Make two cubes from modelling material. The faces should measure about 1 or 1½in, but they must all be the same. Use a ruler to check your measurements.

2 Reshape one of the cubes to form a tall, square-based pyramid. Its base must be the same size as the original cube. You now have a cube and a pyramid.

3 Now measure the cube and pyramid. They have the same volume and the same size base. The pyramid is three times taller, but is strong and more stable.

4 Make the cube into a long slabs. Place the slab and the pyramid on a book. Slowly tilt the book, to imitate the effect of an earthquake. The slab topples over before the pyramid does.

5 Make another smaller cube and pyramid from modeling material. Make sure that they are the same height. Their bases must also be the same size.

6 Do the same book test with the two smaller shapes. You should still find that the pyramid is the more stable of the two shapes. It is the second of the two shapes to fall over.

A question of strength

YOU WILL NEED

Bases and heights: nonhardening modeling material, plastic modeling knife, ruler, book.

A question of strength:

20 large, plastic drinking straws, reusable adhesive.

1 For this project, you will need two models—a cube and a square-based pyramid. Make them out of large plastic drinking straws and reusable adhesive. First, make the cube.

2 After fixing four straws to make the base of your cube, you need eight more to finish it. Make sure that your cube is even, with each face the same size.

3 Now make a square-based pyramid. The base should be the same size as the base of your cube. Make the base, and just fix four more straws to it to complete your pyramid.

4 Push down gently with your hand over the center of the cube. Move your hand slightly to one side as you push down, and you will feel the cube start to collapse.

5 Repeat this with the pyramid. You can feel how much more rigid this shape is, and it does not collapse. This is because a pyramid has triangular-shaped faces that meet at a central point.

Surveying a site

Making precise measurements in order to put up a building is called surveying. Accurate building requires two things. There must be a level base to the building, and building slabs must be laid absolutely flat, with their sides perfectly vertical, at right angles to the ground. Builders use plumb lines to check that verticals are absolutely true. A plumb line is a weight on the end of a line, which holds the line straight. These experiments show how to use water levels or a plumb line to measure differences in heights on a site.

▲ **The lie of the land**
A modern surveyor makes a detailed examination of the land before building work can start.

Is it vertical?

1 Make your own plumb line by fixing a 1¼in ball of modeling material to a piece of string. Make a large knot in the string and model the material around it.

2 Push your stick into the ground. Make it as vertical as possible (pointing straight upward). Keep moving it slightly, until you are sure it is straight.

3 Now use your plumb line to check how straight your stick is. Get a friend to hold the line next to the stick. Measure between the stick and line at the top and farther down. If the measurements are the same, your stick is vertical.

Is your site level?

YOU WILL NEED

Is it vertical?: nonhardening modeling material, string, a stick (about 1 yard long), tape measure.

Is your site level?: wooden stick 1 yard long, plank of wood 16 x 4in, nails, hammer, screw-in hooks, clear plastic piping (about ½in diameter), pitcher, water colored with ink, funnel, tape measure, wooden pole 1 yard long, pen.

1 Here, you are making a simple version of a surveyor's level. To start, nail the short plank of wood to the top of the long wooden stick. Take care with the hammer.

2 Now screw the hooks in along the bottom and up the sides of the plank. Thread the piping through the hooks. About ¾in of piping should stick up above the plank.

3 Get a friend to hold the device upright. Now, very carefully, pour the water into the pipe, using a funnel. The water level should come just above the piece of wood.

4 The friend holds the pole up 5 yards away. You look along the water levels so they line up, and also line up with the pole. The friend moves a finger up and down the pole. Shout when the friend's finger lines up with the water levels.

5 The friend marks this on the pole, then moves to another spot. Repeat step 4. The distance between the two marks on the pole shows the difference in level between the two places.

Powerful levers

One of the simplest and oldest gadgets in the world is the lever. Any rod or stick can act as a lever, helping to move heavy objects or prise things apart. Levers are also used for lifting, cutting, and squashing. The action of a lever can make a push more forceful, or make it a smaller push. It can also change the direction of a push. The difference between the size of the push you make on a lever (the effort) and the push the lever itself makes (the load) is called mechanical advantage.

A lever on a central pivot can also be used as a balance. The lever balances if the effect of the force (push) on one side of the pivot is the same as the effect of the force on the other. A seesaw is one sort of balancing lever. It is a plank balanced on a central post or pivot. A big person can balance someone small and light if they sit nearer to the central pivot of the seesaw.

▲ Using a simple lever

A spoon can be a lever. This girl is using the spoon as a simple lever to lift the lid off a can of paint. The lever arm pivots on the lip of the can. As the girl pushes down on the long end, the shorter end wedged under the lid lifts it up with greater force, making the stiff lid move.

▲ Cracking a nut

The strong crushing action of the nutcracker's jaws is produced by pressing the two lever arms together. A pair of nutcrackers, like a pair of scissors or a pair of pliers, has two lever arms joined at a pivot. The levers make the effort you use about four times bigger, allowing you to break the nut easily. Putting the pivot at the end of the nutcracker rather than toward the center (as in a pair of scissors), means that the arms of the cracker can be shorter, but still create a force just as big.

lever arm

jaws

pivot

effort

load

pivot

▲ Body levers

Did you know that some parts of your body are levers? Every time you brush your hair or get up from a chair, the bones in your arms and legs act as levers. As your arm lifts up an object, your elbow is the pivot. Effort from the upper arm is transferred to your lower arm, so that you can pick up the load in your hand.

Levers and lifting

I A ruler can be used as a lever to lift a book. With the pivot (the box) near the book, only a small effort is needed to lift the book up. The lever makes the push greater.

effort

load

pivot

▲ How a lever works

A lever tilts on a pivot, which is nearer to the end of the lever with the load on it. The effort, or force, is the push you make on the long end of the lever to lift the weight of the load.

2 When the pivot is moved to the middle of the lever, the effort needed to lift the book up is equal to the book's weight. The effort and the load are the same.

3 When the pivot is near where you are pressing, more effort is needed to lift the book. The force of the push needed to lift the book is now larger than the book's weight.

Balancing a seesaw

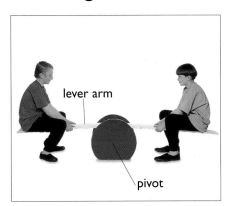

lever arm

pivot

I Ask a friend of equal weight to sit on one side of the seesaw, while you sit on the other side. If you sit the same distance from the pivot, you make the seesaw balance.

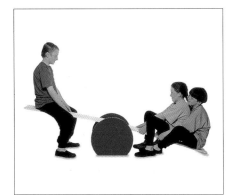

2 Ask another friend to join you on the seesaw. By adding another person, that side of the seesaw will overbalance. The pair's greater weight will easily lift the lighter person.

3 Get the pair to move nearer to the pivot of the seesaw. Their weight can be balanced by the lighter person moving farther away from the pivot. The seesaw will be equally balanced.

Levers at work

Find out how to make three different kinds of lever in these experiments. The first is a can crusher that uses a lever action to squash a can. The second is a gripper for picking up small objects, just like a pair of tweezers. It can also work as a nutcracker. In a pair of nutcrackers, the load (in this case a candy or a nut) is between the pivot (the pencil) and the effort (where you push). In a pair of tweezers, the effort is between the pivot and the load.

The third experiment is a balance scale. It is like the ones used by the Romans about 2,000 years ago. It works by balancing the weight of an object against a known weight, in this case a bag of coins. The coins are moved along the lever arm, until they balance the object being weighed. The farther away from the pivot the weighed bag is, the greater turning effect it has on the lever arm. The heavier the weight being measured, the farther away the bag must be moved to balance the arm. The weight is read against the scale along the arm.

YOU WILL NEED

two short planks of wood about 16 x 4in and ½–¾in thick, hinge, screws, screwdriver, two coffee-jar lids, glue, empty can.

Can crusher

1 Lay the two planks of wood end to end. Ask an adult to help you screw them together with a hinge, using screws and a screwdriver. Make sure the hinge is secure.

2 Glue a jar lid to the inside edge of each plank of wood, with the top of the lid face down. The lids should be about halfway along each plank and the same distance from the hinge.

To crush a can, put the can in between the lids, so that it is held in place. Press down hard on the top piece of wood.

148

Gripper

1 Put the pencil between the two pieces of wood, near one end. Wrap the rubber bands tightly around the pieces of wood to make a pivot. You have now made the gripper.

2 Hold the gripper near the pivot to make it act like a pair of tweezers. See if you can pick up a delicate object, such as a candy or a grape, without crushing the object.

3 Hold the gripper at the end farthest away from the pivot. Now your lever operates as a pair of nutcrackers. The effort at the point you push is increased.

Balance scale

YOU WILL NEED

Gripper: short pencil, two pieces of wood each about 6in long, thick rubber bands, objects to pick up or squash, such as candies or nuts.

Balance scale: thick card about 20 x 3in, thin card, scissors, string, ruler, hole punch, 4½in circle of card, tape, 4oz of coins, felt-tipped pen, objects to weigh.

1 Make the arm by folding the thick card in two. Make a loop of thin card and fold it loosely around the arm 4¼in from one end. Tie a piece of string to this support.

2 Make a hole ½in from the arm's end. Make the card circle into a cone. Tie it to the hole. Make an envelope from thin card, and tie it to a loop so that it hangs over the arm.

3 Put the coins in the envelope and seal it up. Starting from the middle of the support, make a mark every 2in along the arm. This scale will tell you the weight of an object.

To weigh an object, put it in the cone and slide the envelope of coins backward and forward along the arm, until the arm balances. Each mark along the scale equals 2oz. In this picture, the object being weighed is about 3oz.

149

The power of energy

Nothing can happen without energy. Energy is needed to do work, such as making things move. To make something move, a source of energy is needed. For example, an engine works by burning fuel—a storage of chemical energy. The two experiments here explore different ways in which energy can be captured to make something move.

The turbine experiment shows how the energy in flowing water makes a bottle spin. This energy is used in hydroelectric power stations to generate electricity. The second project shows how electrical energy from a battery spins a motor. Electric motors are used in many household appliances, such as vacuum cleaners and washing machines.

The development of the steam engine and the electric motor in the 1800s provided new sources of energy that were able to power ships and railway engines, for example, and later, to light homes and streets.

▲ **Strike a light**
Lightning is a massive discharge of energy from a thundercloud. The cloud gets overloaded with electrically charged particles of water and ice.

YOU WILL NEED

scissors, plastic bottle, pencil, two wide drinking straws, plastic tape, thin string, tray, water.

3 Hold your turbine over a tray, or outdoors, so that you will not make a mess with the water. Fill the bottle with water. It will squirt out through the straws, making the bottle spin.

Turbine

1 Cut off the bottle's top. Use the pencil to poke holes around its base. Cut the straws and push them through the holes. Use tape to hold the straws in place.

2 Poke three holes around the top of the bottle. Tie three equal pieces of string through the holes, and join them to one long piece of string.

Electric motor

1 Use the bradawl to make a hole ½in from the top of each of the two end supports. Glue them to the base board, ½in inward from the shorter edges.

2 Cut a length of straw 4½in long. Glue the straw to one coil support. Glue the two coil support spacers to either side of the straw. Glue the second support over the top.

3 Strip ¾in of insulation from one end of the wire and 1¼in from the other. Wind wire between the coil supports. Slide the reel onto the straw, with the longest part of the straw showing.

6 Place the magnets on the supports, so that the coil and reel spin freely. Unbend two paper clips to make hooks. Join one end of each to a connecting wire and fix to the base with thick tape. Using paper clips, join the ends of the wires to the battery. The reel should start spinning around.

4 Cut a foil strip the width of the reel, to fit three-quarters of the way around the reel. Cut it in half. Put the wire ends against the reel. Tape foil over each wire so it is under the foil's center.

5 Stick the reel to the straw. Hold it between the end supports. Slide the knitting needle through the hole in each end support. Secure the coil support with green magnet supports.

Wind and water power

Modern windmills called wind turbines are used to generate electricity. The most efficient wind turbines only have two or three blades, like the propeller of an aircraft. Sometimes just a couple of large turbines can generate enough electricity to meet all the power needs of a small community.

There are several shapes of wind turbine. One of the most efficient is the vertical-axis type. This has an axle like the dowel one in the first project. It is very efficient, because it works no matter which way the wind is blowing. The second experiment shows you how to make a water wheel that captures the energy of falling water to lift a small weight. Pour water from different heights to see if it makes a difference to the wheel's speed.

sails

simple gears

grinding stones

▲ Wind for milling

A windmill uses the power of the wind to turn heavy mill stones that grind grain to make flour. The whole building can be turned around, so that it faces into the wind. The speed of the mill is controlled by opening and closing slots in the sails. Inside a windmill is an arrangement of gear wheels, which transfers power from the sails to the grinding stones.

To make the windmill spin, hold it vertically with your fingers on the thumb tacks at each end of the dowel. Blow on the vanes. The windmill will spin easily.

YOU WILL NEED

plastic bottle, scissors, tape, ruler, thin dowel, thumb tacks.

Make a windmill

1 Cut the top and bottom off the bottle to leave a tube. Cut the tube in half lengthwise, then stick the two halves together in an S shape, so that the edges overlap by ¾in.

2 The piece of dowel should be about 1½in longer than the vanes. Slide it into the slot between the vanes. Press a thumb tack gently into each end of the dowel.

Make a water-wheel

1 Cut the top third off the plastic
bottle. Cut a small hole in the
bottom piece near the base (this is to
let the water out). Cut a V-shape on
each side of the rim.

2 Ask an adult to push the wire
through the center of the cork to
make an axle. From the top third of
the plastic bottle, cut six small curved
vanes (blades) as shown.

3 Ask an adult to cut six slots in the
cork with a craft knife. (This might
be easier without the wire.) Push the
plastic vanes into the slots to make
the water wheel.

5 Put the water wheel on
a large plate or in the
sink. Pour water onto the
wheel, so that it hits the
upward-curving vanes. As
the wheel turns, the weight
should be
lifted up.

4 Rest the wheel's axle in the
V-shaped slots. Tape a piece of
string toward one end of the axle, and
tie a small weight to the end of the
string. Fill a pitcher with water.

Energy from liquid and air

Hydraulic machines have parts that are moved by liquid. Pneumatic machines have parts that are moved by a gas such as air. A hydraulic system has a pipe filled with a liquid, such as oil, and a piston that moves to and fro within the pipe. Pushing liquid into the pipe forces the piston to move, transmitting power from one end of the pipe to the other. In a simple pneumatic system, compressed air forces a piston to move.

In the first experiment, you make a simple hydraulic machine powered by water pressure. Water is poured from a central reservoir (the pitcher of water) into a pipe. The water fills up a plastic bag. The bag expands and forces up the piston (the lid), which in turn raises a heavy object. Many cranes and trucks use this principle to lift heavy loads. In the air pump project, you discover the basic principles of how vacuum cleaners work. Finally, you make a miniature vacuum cleaner. Air is sucked in one hole and pushed out of another. A valve stops it from being sucked in and pushed out of the wrong holes.

◄ Filling an empty space

Modern vacuum cleaners have an air pump operated by an electric motor. The pump creates a vacuum inside the cleaner. Dust rushes in from the outside to fill the vacuum.

YOU WILL NEED

large plastic bottle, scissors, airtight plastic bag, plastic tube, tape, plastic funnel, spray can lid, heavy book, pitcher of water.

Make an hydraulic lifter

1 Cut the top off the large plastic bottle. Make sure the plastic bag is airtight, and wrap its neck over the end of a piece of plastic tube. Seal the bag to the tube with tape.

2 Fix a funnel to the other end of the tube. Make a hole at the base of the bottle, and feed the bag and tube through. The bag should sit in the bottom of the bottle.

3 Put the spray can lid on top of the bag, and rest a heavy book on top of the bottle. Lift the funnel end of the tube up, and slowly pour in water. What happens to the lid and the book?

Make an air pump

1 Cut around the large plastic bottle, about one third up from the bottom. Cut a slit down the side of the bottom part of the bottle, so that it will slide inside the top part.

2 Ask an adult to help you nail the bottom of the bottle to the end of a wooden stick or a piece of dowel. You have now made a piston for your air pump.

3 Cut a hole about ½in across near the neck of the bottle. Cut a piece of card about ¾ x ¾in. Tape one edge of the card to the bottle to form a flap over the hole.

4 Drop a ping-pong ball into the top part of the bottle, so that it rests in the neck. Push the bottom part of the bottle (the piston) into the top part (the cylinder).

5 Move the piston in and out, to suck air into the bottle and out of the hole. Can you see how both the valves work? The flap should automatically close when you pull the piston out.

Make a vacuum cleaner

1 Make the air pump from the project above without the card flap. Tape string to the ball, feed it through the bottle's neck, and tape it down, so that the ball is held near the neck.

2 Make a tissue paper bag and glue it over the hole near the neck of the bottle. Air from the pump will go through the bag, and anything the vacuum picks up should be trapped.

3 Try picking up tiny bits of paper with the vacuum. Pull the piston out sharply to suck the bits of paper into the bottle. Push the piston back in gently to pump the paper into the bag.

How magnets work

Magnets are usually made of the metal iron, or another material that has lots of iron in it, such as steel. Magnets can be various shapes, but all of them have the ability to pull things toward themselves. This invisible force is called magnetism. Magnets only attract (pull) metals that are made of iron or that contain iron.

Magnetism is concentrated around the poles (ends) of a magnet. A magnet has two poles, called the north pole and the south pole. The two poles may look the same but they behave differently. Put one pole of a magnet near to a pole of another magnet, and watch what happens. You may feel an attraction (pulling) force as the two poles stick together. Alternatively, you may feel a repulsion (pushing) force, as the two poles push away from each other. In all magnets, identical poles will repel (push away) each other, while different poles will pull towards each other.

Is a big magnet more powerful than a small one? Not always. You cannot tell how powerful a magnet is just by looking at it. Compare the strength and power of different magnets in the projects opposite.

▲ Seeing magnetism

You cannot see the magnetic force around a magnet, but you can see the effects of its presence when an iron nail sticks to a magnet. You can see the shape of a magnetic field by using tiny, powderlike pieces of iron, called iron filings. Iron filings reveal that the lines and strength of the magnetic force are concentrated around and between the poles at the end of the horseshoe magnet. On a bar magnet, they line up to show how the magnetic force spreads out from the poles (ends).

Tiny magnets ▶

Think of a bar of iron as having millions of micromagnets inside it. These are called domains. If they are all jumbled up, the bar is not a magnet. If the micromagnets in a bar are lined up and point the same way, it is a magnet.

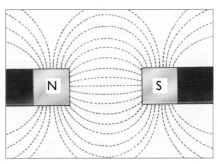

◀ Attraction and repulsion ▶

The poles of two magnets that are different or opposite will attract. Magnetic lines of force from north and south poles pull together and join. The poles of two magnets that are the same will repel or push each other apart.

Strength of a magnet

1 Cut off a piece of tape and use it to tape the round container firmly to the work surface. The round container will act as the pivot, or the balancer.

2 Attach a magnet to one end of the ruler with a rubber band and some washers to the other end of the ruler. Position the middle of the ruler on the balancer.

3 Hold another magnet above the first. Lower it until the ruler tips over. Measure its height above the table. The higher it is when the ruler tips over, the stronger the magnet.

YOU WILL NEED

Strength of a magnet: scissors, tape, round plastic container, two magnets, ruler, rubber bands, steel washers.

Power of a magnet: pencil, thumb tacks, strong thread, card, ruler with holes at both ends and in the middle, scissors, tape, rubber bands, adhesive dots, pen, two small bar magnets.

Power of a magnet

1 Attach one end of a piece of thread to a tack and the other to a pencil. Draw two large quarter-circles on card. The distance from the pin to curved edge should be as long as the ruler.

2 Draw a triangle in one quarter-circle and cut it out. Using the triangle as a template, cut out a triangle from the other quarter-circle. Tape them together.

3 Push a tack through the ruler's end hole, so that it pivots. Attach rubber bands from the ruler's middle hole to the quarter-circle's side. Add dots labeled N and S to each ruler end.

Stand the magnet measurer upright. Attach one magnet to the ruler's top end with a rubber band. Bring the unlike pole of another magnet near it. How far can it pull the ruler? Stronger magnets pull it farther.

Magnetic Earth

The Earth behaves as if there is a giant bar magnet running through its middle from pole to pole. This affects every magnetic material that comes within its reach. If you hold a magnet so that it can rotate freely, it always ends up with one end pointing to the Earth's North Pole and the other to the South Pole. This is how a compass works—the needle automatically swings to the North. The Earth's magnetism comes from its inner core of iron and nickel.

You can use the compass you make here to plot a magnetic field like the Earth's. The Earth's magnetic field is slightly tilted, so compasses do not swing exactly toward the North Pole, but to a point a little way off from northern Canada. This direction is known as magnetic north.

solar wind · North Pole · lines of magnetic force

tail of magnetosphere blown outward by solar wind

South Pole · Earth

▲ Magnetic protection

The effects of Earth's magnetism extend 37,000 miles out into space. In fact, there is a vast magnetic force field around the Earth called the magnetosphere. This traps electrically charged particles and so protects the Earth from the solar wind—the deadly stream of charged particles hurtling from the Sun.

Make a compass

1 To turn the needle into a magnet, stroke the end of the magnet slowly along it. Repeat this in the same direction for about 45 seconds. This magnetizes the needle.

2 Place the magnetized needle on the slice of cork. Make sure that it is exactly in the middle, otherwise it will not spin evenly. Tape the needle into place.

3 Fill the bowl nearly to the brim with water, and float the cork in it. Make sure the cork is exactly in the middle and can turn without rubbing on the edges of the bowl.

The Earth's magnetic field should now swivel the needle on the cork. One end of the needle will always point to the north. That end is its north pole.

Magnetic field

1 Lay a large sheet of paper on a table. Put the magnet in the middle of the paper. Set up your needle compass an inch or two away from one end of the magnet.

2 Wait as the compass needle settles in a particular direction as it is swiveled by the magnet. Make a pencil mark on the paper to show which way it is pointing.

3 Move the compass a little way toward the other end of the magnet. Mark a line on the paper to show which way the needle is pointing now.

4 Repeat Step 3 for about 25 different positions around the magnet. Try the compass both near the magnet and farther away. You should now have a pattern of marks.

Look at the pattern of marks you have made on the paper. They should form a series of rings around the magnet, like layers of an onion. Earth's magnetic field is shaped like this.

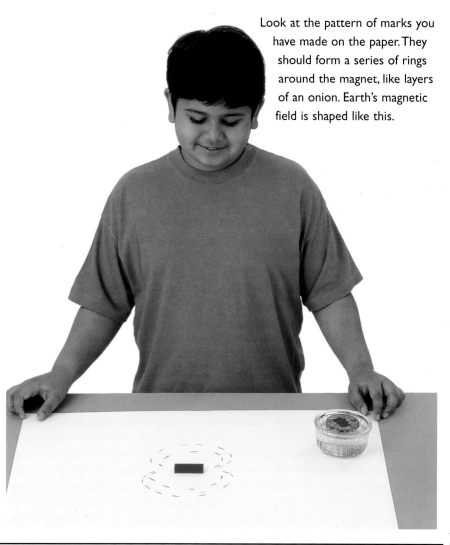

Magnets and maps

Look at a map—which way up does it go? Maps are important. They let us know our location. Without magnets, we would not know how to use a map or find our way around an area. Compass needles are tiny magnets that rotate to point to the Earth's magnetic north. Look on a local map to find a diagram of the compass points, an arrow, or 'N' that indicates north. Then set a compass so that the needle points north. Turn the map so that its north faces the same way as the compass north. Now the map is lined up accurately in relation to the landscape. If you are on a hilltop with wide views, you can see how the map is a tiny plan of the countryside around.

▲ Magnetic migration

The yellow arrows show the migration routes of the Arctic tern. The routes follow the Earth's magnetic force. The tern flies from north to south and then, later in the year, from south to north. Birds may also use rivers, mountains, coastlines, the Sun, Moon, and stars to help them find their way.

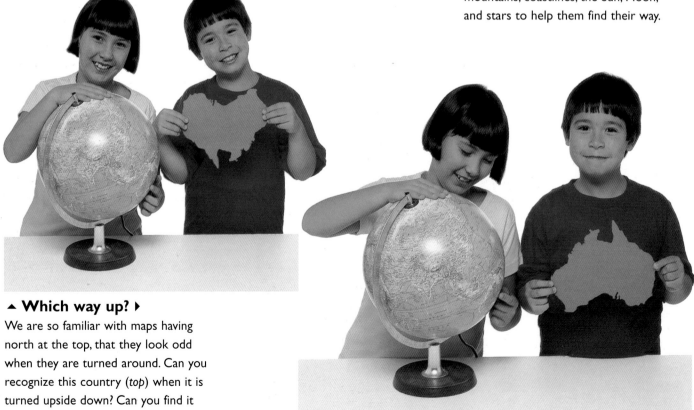

▲ Which way up? ▶

We are so familiar with maps having north at the top, that they look odd when they are turned around. Can you recognize this country (*top*) when it is turned upside down? Can you find it on the globe (*right*)?

Loop compass

1 Straighten out a paper clip. Magnetize it by stroking it with the strong magnet. Cut a disk of card, bend the wire into a large loop, and insert it into holes in the card.

2 Tape the paper clip to the piece of cork and to the card circle. Tie the thread to the top of the wire loop. Let it hang and twirl around freely. It is now ready to test.

3 Does the paper clip magnet work as a compass needle and point north and south? Check it with the store-bought compass. What do you find happens?

Drawing a maze

YOU WILL NEED

Loop compass: paper clip, strong magnet, card, scissors, thin wire, tape, cork tile, thread, store-bought compass.

Drawing a maze: cardboard, colored pens, compass.

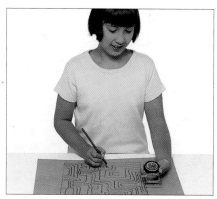

1 Draw a maze on cardboard. Make it colorful and fun. Put in some dead ends and false turns. Make sure one route leads all the way through from one end of the maze to another!

2 Record your course through the maze, using compass points for the direction. You can limit the information to north, south, east, and west or include northeast, southwest and so on.

Can you find your way through this maze? When you have made it to the other side, try recording your route with compass points. At the beginning of the journey, you head east, turn north and then go east again. Can you complete these instructions for the entire journey?

OUT

IN

N

W E

S

Electric magnets

Some magnets, such as bar and horseshoe magnets, are permanent. They have what scientists call "spontaneous permanent magnetism." Their magnetism needs no outside force or energy to create it. A way of making magnetism is by using electricity. When electricity flows through a wire or another similar conducting (carrying) material, it produces a magnetic field around the wire. This is called electromagnetism or EM. In fact, magnetism and electricity are very closely linked. Each can be used to make the other. EM is used in many tools, machines, and devices. Some electromagnetic machines use the electricity from batteries. Others need the much more powerful mains electricity from wall sockets.

The first practical electromagnets were made by the British bootmaker and spare-time scientist, William Sturgeon. He used them to amaze audiences at his science shows in the 1820s. The basic design has hardly changed since. You can make a similar electromagnet in the projects.

wires carrying electricity
case   wire coil
magnet
frame
moving cone

▲ Loudspeaker

Electrical signals are transferred to the loudspeaker along a connecting wire (speaker lead). Electricity flows through the wire coil, which is attached to the plastic speaker cone. The signals make the coil into an electromagnet that varies in strength. This magnetic field is itself inside the field of a strong permanent magnet. The two fields interact, with like poles repelling. This makes the coil move or vibrate, and the loudspeaker cone vibrates, too. This in turn sends out sound waves.

▶ Creating a magnetic field

As electricity flows through a wire, a magnetic field is created around it. The magnetic lines of force flow in circles around the wire. This is called an electromagnetic field. As soon as the electricity is switched off, the magnetism stops.

◀ Seeing electromagnetism

If iron filings are sprinkled onto a piece of cardboard that has an electricity-carrying wire through it, the filings are affected by the magnetic field. They arrange themselves in circles to show the lines of magnetic force, as they do with an ordinary magnet.

▼ Are you receiving me?

The earpiece of a telephone receives varying electrical signals from the mouthpiece of the telephone held at other end of the line. The earpiece works like a simple loudspeaker to recreate the sounds of the speaking person's voice.

diaphragm (thin sheet)
magnets
wire coil

Electromagnet

1 Using the wire strippers, carefully remove an inch or two of plastic insulation from each end of the wire. These bare ends will connect to the battery.

2 Carefully wrap the wire into a tight coil around the iron nail. The plastic insulation around the wire conducts the electricity around the iron nail.

3 Connect the wire's ends to the battery terminals. (It does not matter which is positive or negative.) Test your electromagnet by picking up paper clips.

Adding a switch

YOU WILL NEED

Electromagnet: wire strippers, 2 yards of wire (insulated, plastic-coated, multistrand copper), large iron nail, 9-volt battery, paper clips.

Adding a switch: hole punch piece of card, brass fasteners.

screen

electrical plates have a magnetic field

electron guns

beam is bent by field

▲ Inside a television

Television sets, computer monitors, and other similar screens have electromagnet-type devices inside. These are usually shaped like flat plates. They bend the beam that scans across the screen line by line, to build up the picture. This occurs many times every second.

1 Make two equal-sized holes in the piece of card. Push the brass fasteners into them. Push one of the fasteners through a paper clip first. Open out the legs of the fasteners.

2 Connect one end of electromagnet wire to the fastener. Connect the other to a battery terminal. Attach the remaining fastener to the other terminal with short wire. Turn the card over.

WARNING!
NEVER use electricity from wall sockets. It is too dangerous and could kill you. Ask an adult for help with this project.

3 Push the paper clip attached to one fastener away from the other fastener. No electricity flows. Turn the clip to touch the fastener. Electricity flows, switching on the electromagnet.

Computer data storage

The hard disk of a computer consists of a number of flat, circular plates. Each one of these plates is coated with tiny magnetic particles. The hard disk also contains a controlling mechanism called the read/write head. This is positioned slightly above the magnetic plates. Data (information) is sent to the disk as a series of electrical pulses. These are sent to the read/write head, which contains a tiny electromagnet. The head magnetizes the tiny magnetic particles on the surface of the plates. This pattern of particles on the disk represents the data. You can see how this happens in the project.

When reading information, the magnetized particles on the hard disk create a small current in the head as the plates spin under it. This is then converted by circuits into binary code, a number system that computers use. The code is based on just two numbers (binary means two), 0 and 1. Different combinations represent the letters of the alphabet.

central point around which the disks spin

read/write he

magnetic plates store information

hard drive inside the computer

▲ Inside the hard drive

A typical drive consists of a stack of thin disks, called a platter. The upper surface of each disk is coated with tiny magnetic particles, and each disk has its own read/write head on a movable arm. When storing and reading information, the disks spin at very high speeds (up to 100 revolutions a second).

Input devices

mouse

keyboard

scanner

Storage devices

hard drive

CD-ROMS

zip disk

Processing

Output devices

printer

monitor

speakers

◀ Using computers

When people use a computer, they are doing four different things:

1. Inputting data (information) using an input device.

2. Storing the data so that it can be reused (often called data storage).

3. Working with the data they put in (often called processing).

4. Retrieving and looking at the data using an output device.

Make your own viewer

1 Use a pair of sharp scissors to cut a small square hole, approximately ¾ x ¾in, in one end of the cardboard box. You may need an adult's help to do this.

2 Now cut a much larger square hole in the other end of your cardboard box. Cut out most of the end of the box, as shown in the picture.

3 Cut a square of thin card about 1½ x 1½in. Find the center of the card using a ruler. Use a sharp pencil to pierce a tiny hole in the center of the card.

4 Place the piece of thin card over the outside of the smaller hole on the box. Make sure that the pencil hole is centerd over the square hole. Now tape it into place.

5 Cut a square of tracing paper slightly bigger than the larger hole at the other end of the box. Stick it securely over that hole. Your viewer is now ready to use.

6 Look out of a window, through the screen of tracing paper. Try tracing the image you see onto the paper.

pencil hole

tracing paper screen

When you use your viewer, the pencil hole lets in just a few light rays from each part of the scene. The rays keep going in straight lines and hit the tracing paper screen, making an upside-down image of the scene.

A photographic image

The camera's job is to create a focused image of a scene, but this would be no use without a way of recording the image. This is the job of the film. There are three basic types of film—color negative, color-reversal, and black and white. Film comes in different sizes (called formats) and lengths. Most cameras take 35mm film, and the usual lengths are 24 and 36 exposures.

Film is coated with a chemicals that are affected by light. When an image strikes the film, the coating records the patterns of light, dark, and color. Film has to be developed with chemicals before you can see the recorded pictures. Until then, it must be kept in complete darkness. When undeveloped film is exposed to direct light, it turns black.

This project shows that you do not need to have a camera to see how film works. In fact, you do not even need a film! You can use black and white photographic paper instead. Photographic paper is the paper that prints are made on. It works in the same way as film. Here, you can see how to make a picture called a photogram. It is made by covering some parts of a sheet of photographic paper with objects and then shining light on the sheet. When the paper is developed, the areas that were hit by the light turn black, leaving you an image of the objects.

▲ Danger!
This symbol, on photographic chemical bottles, means that they can be dangerous if not used with care. Always wear protective gloves and goggles.

◀ Photographic paper
For black and white prints, you need a paper called monochrome paper. Buy the smallest size you can, and choose grade 2 if possible, with a gloss (shiny) finish. The paper comes in a light-proof envelope or box. Only open the envelope in complete darkness. The paper is in a second, black polyurethene envelope. You will also need two photographic chemicals—developer for paper (not film) and fixer. Buy them from a photographic supplier, and ask an adult to help you use them safely.

Make your own photogram

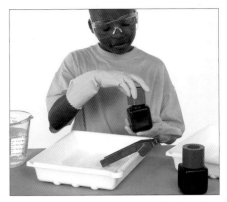

1 Ask an adult to help you follow the instructions to dilute the chemicals with water. Protect your eyes and hands when handling them. Store the diluted chemicals in plastic bottles.

2 Turn off the lamp. Lay a sheet of photographic paper down, shiny side up. Put some objects on it. Then turn the lamp on again for a few seconds.

3 Pick up the paper with the tongs, and put it into the dish of developer. Push the paper down, so that it is completely underneath the liquid.

4 After a minute, use the tongs to move the paper into the fixer. Leave the paper right under the liquid for a minute, until the image is fixed.

images made on photographic paper

5 Now you can turn the light back on. Using the tongs, lift the paper out of the fixer and wash it with running water for a few minutes. Then lay the paper on a flat surface to dry. This technique is an excellent way of producing unique invitations and greetings cards quickly and effectively.

Getting in focus

Before taking a photograph, you need to make sure that your subject is in focus. When it is, all the rays of light that leave a point on the subject are bent by the lens, so that they hit the correct place on the film. This makes a clear, sharp image. Parts of the scene inside or behind the subject may not be in focus. On some cameras, you have to choose the part of the scene that you want to be in focus. Autofocus cameras focus the lens by automatically choosing the object at the center of the image to be taken.

This experiment involves making a simple camera with just a few basic pieces of equipment. It uses photographic paper (paper with a light-sensitive coating on one side) instead of film, and a pinhole instead of a lens. When the paper is processed, you will have a negative. The "Easy prints" project on the next page shows you how to develop it.

YOU WILL NEED

pinhole box viewer, aluminum foil, scissors, tape, pencil, black paper, thin card, ruler, heavy light-proof cloth or plastic sheet, photographic paper, rubber band.

viewfinder

lens *pentaprism*

light ray *mirror*

▲ Focusing SLRs

With an SLR (single lens reflex) camera, you can see exactly what the image looks like through the viewfinder. On a manual-focus SLR, you turn a ring around the lens until your subject comes into focus. When the subject is in focus, the light rays meet on the film focal plane. This is the exposed part of the film that is held flat at the back of the camera by a pressure plate. You can see it if you open the back of your camera when it is empty.

◀ Get it sharp

In this photograph (*left*), the subject is in sharp focus. You can see all the fine detail. When the same shot is out of focus (*below*), it makes the subject look blurred. Autofocus cameras focus on the object in the middle of the viewfinder and do the job of focusing for you.

Making a pinhole camera

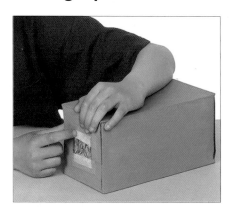

1 Make the pinhole viewer from the "Make your own viewer" project, but remove the tracing-paper screen. Replace the 1½in card square with aluminum foil.

2 Pierce a hole, about ⅟₁₆in across, in the middle of the foil using a sharp pencil. Open the back of the box. Roll up some black paper, and fit it through the large hole to line the inside.

Sound waves

1 Place the watch close to your ear. You can hear a ticking sound coming from it. The sound becomes fainter when you move the watch away from your ear.

2 Place one end of the tube over a friend's ear, and hold the watch at the other end. The tube concentrates the sound and does not let it spread out. She can hear the watch clearly.

How to make panpipes

1 Cut the drinking straws so that you have four pairs that are 3½in, 3in, 2½in, and 2in long. Block up one end of each straw with a small piece of modeling material.

2 Carefully cut out the card to the same shape as the blue piece shown above. Fix the straws into place with the tape from long to short, to align with card as shown.

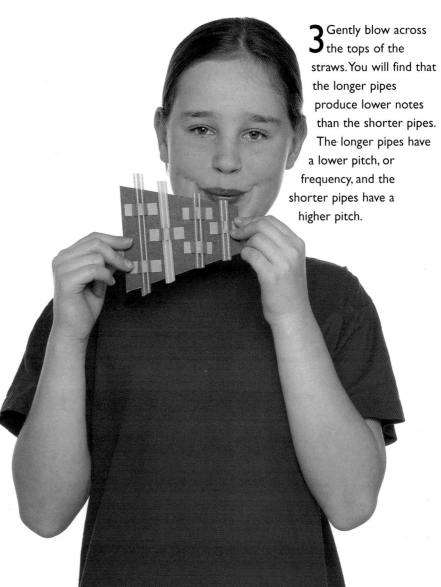

3 Gently blow across the tops of the straws. You will find that the longer pipes produce lower notes than the shorter pipes. The longer pipes have a lower pitch, or frequency, and the shorter pipes have a higher pitch.

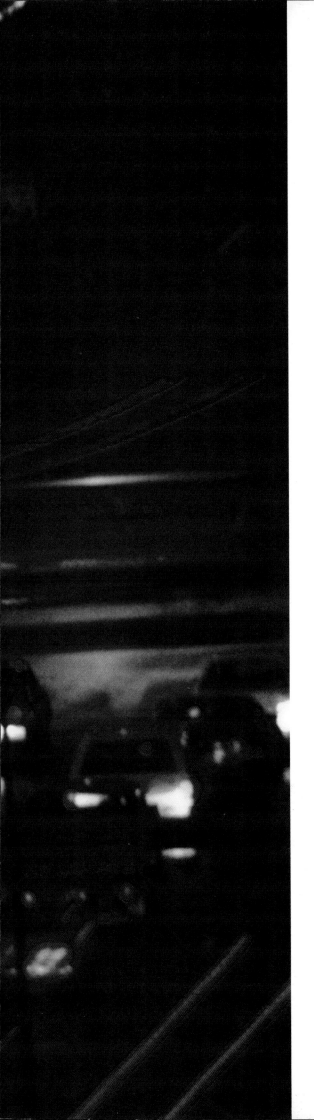

Travel and Transportation

The most powerful, luxurious, and specialized forms of transportation today all evolved from simple scientific principles. The trick of keeping a luxury passenger liner or a massive oil tanker afloat is basically the same as it was for early humans with their canoes and coracles. Many of the secrets of superpowered vehicles are the result of learning to make use of simple forces such as jet propulsion, thrust, and lift, and combining them with other inventions and new materials. On the following pages, you will discover how boats, trains, cars, planes, and spacecraft work by experimenting with the forces that make them go.

Simple boats

Some of the earliest and simplest types of boat are still made today. Small reed boats are still built in southern Iraq and on Lake Titicaca in South America in a similar way to the one in the project below. Reed boats are made by tying thousands of river reeds together into huge bundles. The bundles are then tied together to make hull shapes. In ancient Egypt, large boats were made like this, from papyrus reeds. Some historians believe that Egyptians may have made long ocean crossings in papyrus craft.

The model in the second project is of a coracle. This is a round boat made by covering a light wooden frame with animal hides. Coracles are also still made, but are now covered with canvas treated with tar instead of animal hide. Coracles were small enough for one person to paddle along a river and were used for fishing. When you are out near a river or lake, take photographs or make drawings of other simple craft, such as canoes and punts. See if you can make working models of them, too.

◄ Afterlife evidence

This boat was found in a pit alongside the Great Pyramid of Egypt in 1954. It is believed to have been used as a pharaoh's funeral boat, which ferried the dead pharaoh to the afterlife.

Make a reed craft

1 Make bundles of raffia by tying a few dozen strands together with a short piece of raffia. You will need two bundles about 8in long and two more about 10in long.

2 Tie the two long bundles and the two short bundles together. Tie the short bundles on top of the long ones. Fix a strand between each end, to make the ends bend up.

3 Gently lower the reed boat onto the surface of a tank of water. How well does it float? Does it stay upright? Try leaving it in the water to see if it becomes waterlogged.

Make a coracle

1 Cut one long piece of cane and three short pieces. Using short pieces of string, tie all three of the short pieces of cane to the long piece to make a triple-armed cross.

2 Cut a much longer piece of cane. Form it into a loop, and tie it to all the ends of the triple cross shape. Bend the ends of the cross up as you tie them to form a dish shape.

3 Cut pieces of cotton cloth about 6 x 2in. Apply glue to the outside of the frame, and place the pieces over it. Glue the pieces to each other where they overlap.

4 Glue down the cloth where it folds over the top of the frame. Put two coats of glue on the outside of the cloth to waterproof it. Leave the glue to dry completely.

When the model is dry, put the finished coracle into a tank of water. How well does it float? Why not try making a person from modeling material to sit in your model coracle?

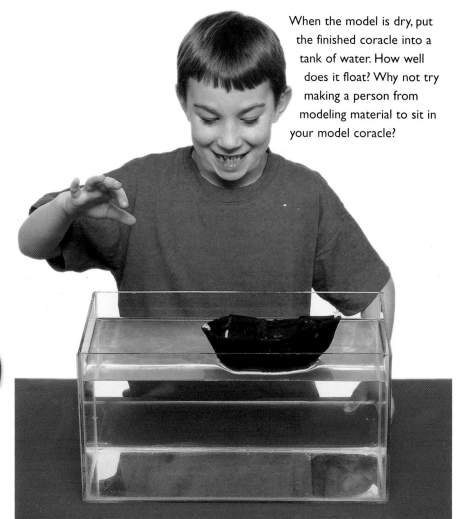

Early Britons used coracles 9,000 years ago. Coracles are light to carry, easy to use, and stable enough to fish from.

Sail power

When you launch your model sailing boat, you can get an idea of how it is propelled by the wind. To sail in the direction they want to go, sailors must be aware of wind direction, so that they can adjust the position of the sails to make best use of it. If sailing boats face straight into the wind, the sails flap uselessly, and the boat is in a "no-go zone." They can, however, sail into oncoming wind by taking a zigzag course. This is called tacking. The wind blows against one side of the sail to propel the boat diagonally upwind. When the boat changes tack, the wind blows against the other side of the sail, and the boat goes forward on the opposite diagonal. If the wind is blowing from behind the boat, the sail is set at right angles to the boat like an open wing, so that it is filled by the wind.

YOU WILL NEED

pencil, ruler, thick card, scissors, tape, plastic sheet, stapler, bradawl, nonhardening modeling material, thin garden canes, colored paper, plastic straw, small plastic bottle, string, paper clip, sheet of paper.

▲ Parts of a sailboat
Sailboats usually have a crew of two people. A helmsman operates the tiller and the mainsail, and a crew who works the jib and centreboard (which stops the boat from drifting sideways).

Template ▶

Make a sailboat

1 Cut out your hull shape from thick card, using the template above as a guide. Score along the dotted lines with the scissors. Use tape to fasten the sides together.

2 Lay the hull on a plastic sheet. Cut the plastic around the hull, allowing enough to cover the sides and overlap them at the top by 2in. Fold the sheet over the hull and staple it in place.

3 Pierce a hole in the middle of a strip of card a little wider than the hull. Staple in place. Put modeling material under the hole, and push a 12in cane through the hole into it.

4 Cut a sail from colored paper with a base of about 8in. Attach the straw along the side and a garden cane along the bottom with tape. Slip the straw over the mast.

5 Cut an L-shape (about 3in long, 1½in wide at the base and ¾in wide at the top) from the small plastic bottle. Cut the base of the L in half to make two slanted tabs, as shown.

6 Fold back the two tabs of the L-shaped plastic in opposite directions, as shown, and staple them to the stern (back) of the boat. This is the boat's rudder.

7 Cut a piece of string about 8in long. Tape one end to the back of the boom (the cane), and feed the other end through a paper clip attached to the back of the boat.

8 To test out how your sail boat works, make a breeze by waving a large sheet of paper near to the boat. Adjust the string to move the sail into the right position.

When you have finished your boat, you could try making and adding a centerboard. Attach a cardboard oblong at right angles to the bottom of the boat. It will stop your boat from drifting sideways in the wind.

direction of wind

When you test your boat, set the sail in these different positions. Alter the position of the sail by using the string taped to the boom (cane). Follow the arrows shown here to see which way the wind should be blowing from in each case. Try blowing from other directions to see if this makes a difference to your boat.

How ships float

The simplest boats, such as rafts, float because the material they are made of is less dense (lighter) than water. Heavy ships can float, because the water they are floating in pushes upward against them. This pushing force is called upthrust. The first experiment shows that an object will float if the upthrust of the water is great enough to overcome the downward push of the object's weight. The size of the upthrust depends on how much water the object pushes out of the way. When you put an object in water and let it go, it settles into the water, pushing liquid out of the way. The farther it goes in, the more water it pushes away and the more upthrust acts on it. When the upthrust becomes the same as the object's weight, the object floats.

The second project shows you a hollow hull. If you push a light, hollow ball under water, it will spring back up. Upthrust from the water makes a hollow hull float in the same way. The higher the density of water, the greater the upthrust. This means that ships float slightly higher in salt water, since it is more dense than fresh water.

salt water

fresh water

▲ Measuring density

The density of water is measured with a hydrometer. You can make one by putting a lump of modeling material on the end of a straw. Put it in a glass of water, and mark the water level with tape. Now put the straw in an equal amount of salty water. What happens?

Testing upthrust

1 Put the two styrofoam chunks into a large tank of water. They will float well, because their material is so light. Only a small amount of upthrust is needed.

2 Try pushing the chunks under the water. Now you are pushing lots of water aside. Can you feel upthrust pushing back? The bigger chunk will experience more upthrust.

3 A wooden block floats deeper in the water, because wood is more dense (heavier) than styrofoam. A marble sinks, because the upthrust on it is not as great as its weight.

Hollow hulls

1 Put a piece of foil about 8in by 6in into a tank of water. With just the slightest push, it will sink. This is because it does not displace much water, so there is very little upthrust.

2 Lift the sheet of foil out of the water, and dry it carefully with a paper towel. Now mold it into a simple boat shape with your fingers. Take care not to tear the foil.

3 Put your foil boat into the water. It should now float. It will not sink so easily. Its shape pushes aside much more water than it did when it was flat, so the upthrust is greater.

Try filling your foil boat with small objects, such as marbles, for cargo. As you put more marbles in, it will float lower and lower. How many marbles can your boat hold before it sinks?

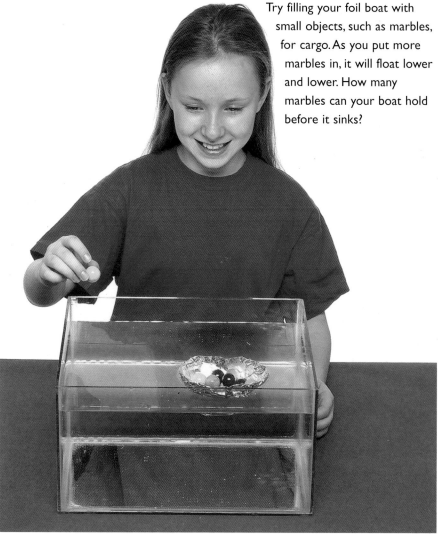

This simple foil boat works like a real ship's hull. Even though it is made of metal, it is filled with air. This gives the hull shape a much lower overall density.

What's in a hull?

Whenever an object such as a ship moves through the water, the water slows it down. The push made by the water is called water resistance, or drag. The faster the object moves, the greater the water resistance becomes.

If you look around a busy harbor, you will see dozens of different hull designs. Sleek, narrow hulls with sharp bows cause less resistance than wide hulls with square bows, so they can move through the water faster.

You can test how the shape of a bow affects the speed of a ship in this experiment. The deeper a hull sits in the water, the more resistance there is. Some hulls are designed to sit just on top of the water. For example, a small speedboat has a flaring, shallow V-shaped hull designed to skim across the surface. A cargo ship has a square hull that sits lower in the water. Speed is not as important for the cargo ship as it is for the speedboat. Instead, the cargo ship is designed for stability, and to carry as much as possible.

Testing hull shapes

I Use a ruler to draw the three templates shown left on sheets of stiff card. Make sure the corners are square and the edges straight. Carefully cut out the shapes.

2 Using scissors, score along the lines inside the base of the square boat (shown as dotted lines left). Bend up the sides, and use tape to fix the corners together.

▲ Templates

Use these three templates to help you cut out and make the three boat shapes in this project.

1¼in

6in

1¼in

4in

1¼in

1¼in

6in

6in

6in

1¼in

6in

4in

3 Make the round-ended and pointed boats in the same way as the first boat. Use a separate piece of card to make the round bow, and tape it to the base in several places.

4 Now cover the outside of each shape with foil, neatly folding the foil over the sides. This will make the shapes more waterproof. Fix a paper clip to the bow (front) of each boat.

5 Roll out three balls of modeling material about the size of a walnut. Weigh the balls to make sure they are the same weight. Attach a ball to the bow of each boat with string.

6 Put a large plastic bowl on a table or a strong box. Use a watering can to pour water into the trough. The water should be about ½in from the top of the bowl.

7 Line up the boats at one end of the bowl. Hang the strings and modeling material balls down over the other end. Put a small wooden brick inside each boat.

Release the boats all at the same time. The weighted strings will pull them along down the length of the bowl. Which one wins the race to the other end of the bowl? Try timing the boats with a stopwatch to work out the difference between the fastest and slowest.

Ship stability

Many ships look as though they are top heavy, so how do they manage to stay upright and not capsize? These projects will help you understand why. When a ship tips over, the hull on that side sinks into the water. On the other side it rises up out of the water. The water creates more upthrust on the side that sinks in, pushing the ship upright again. The more one side of the hull sinks in, the greater the resistance, and the harder it is for the hull to tip over further. A catamaran like the one in the project is extra-stable because it has double hulls against which the water can push.

The position of the cargo in the hull of the ship is important. Heavy cargo high up on deck makes the ship top-heavy and more likely to tip over. Heavy cargo low down in the hull gives the ship stability. Cargo that can move is dangerous, because it could slip to one side of the ship, causing it to tip suddenly. You will be able to test the effects of different weights in square and rounded hulls in the second experiment.

YOU WILL NEED

Make a catamaran: small plastic bottle, scissors, garden cane, rubber bands, tank or bowl of water, cargo.

Loading cargo: plastic bottle and square tub of similar size, scissors, tank or bowl of water, wooden bricks, nonhardening modeling material.

Make a catamaran

I Remove the top from a small plastic bottle, and carefully cut the bottle in half lengthways. This will leave you with two identical shapes to form the catamaran hulls.

Put your completed catamaran into a tank or bowl of water. Load the hulls with cargo such as wooden bricks. Can you make your boat capsize?

2 Place the two halves of the bottle side by side. Lay two medium-length pieces of garden cane on top. Securely fasten the canes to the bottle halves using rubber bands.

3 Attach the two small bottles to both sides of the large bottle using rubber bands. Twist the small bottles so that the small hole on each one points upward.

4 Push a plastic straw into each small hole, so that a bit pokes through. Seal around the base of the straws with modeling material to make a watertight joint.

5 Put a small bulldog clip about halfway down each straw. The clips need to be strong enough to squash the straw and stop air from being forced out by the water.

6 Put your model submarine in a tank of water. With the clips on, it should float. Remove the clips and water will flood the buoyancy tanks. The submarine will sink.

7 To make the submarine surface again, blow slowly into both straws at once. The air will force the water out of the buoyancy tanks, and the submarine will rise to the surface.

This is the finished model submarine. You might find that your model sinks bow (front) first, or stern (back) first. If this is the case, level it by shaking the sand evenly inside the bottle.

8 When your model submarine has resurfaced, keep blowing slowly into the tanks. Replace each bulldog clip and your model submarine will remain floating on the surface.

propeller · stabilizer fin · turbine · aft hydroplane · nuclear reactor · communications antenna · conning tower · periscope · torpedo room · torpedo tube · forward hydroplane · electric motor · missile tube · control room · crew's living quarters · sonar array

▲ Parts of a submarine

A modern submarine, such as this nuclear ballistic missile submarine, is almost as long as a football field—100yd. It has an engine and propeller at the stern, and is operated by a crew of 140. Steam drives the turbines that turn the propeller. A submarine's hull is strong, but few submarines can go below 1,600ft.

Making rails

A full freight or passenger train is heavy, so the track it runs on has to be tough. Nowadays, rails are made from steel, which is a much stronger material than the cast iron used for the first railways. The shape of the rail also helps to make it strong. If you sliced through a rail from top to bottom, you would see it has an "I"-shaped cross section. The broad, flat bottom narrows into the "waist" of the I, and widens again into a curved head. Most countries use a rail shaped like this.

Tracks are made up of pieces of rail, which are laid on wooden or concrete crossbeams called sleepers. Train wheels are a set distance apart, so rails must be a set distance apart, too. The distance between rails is called the gauge. This project will show you how to make sets of railway tracks for the models on the following pages. Make at least two sets of tracks—the more tracks you make, the further your train can travel.

direction of train

rodding cables from points signal box

guard rails guide wheels and avoid derailment

points

points are moved by an electric motor

◀ Points system

Trains are switched from one track to another using points. Part of the track (the blade) moves to guide the wheels smoothly from one route to another. A signaller moves the blades by pulling a lever in the signal box. The blade and the lever are connected by metal rods. The lever cannot be pulled unless the signal is clear.

Making tracks

1 Place one 10¼in x 4¼in piece of card lengthways. Draw a line ½in in from each of the outside edges. Draw two more lines, each 2¼in in from the outside edges. This is side A.

2 Turn the card over (side B) and place it lengthways. Measure and draw lines 1½in and 1¾in in from each edge. Repeat steps 1 and 2 with the second piece of 10¼in x 4¼in card.

3 Hold the ruler firmly against one of the lines you have drawn. Use the tip of a pair of scissors to score along the line. Repeat for all lines on both sides of both pieces of card.

4 Place the cards A side up. For each piece in turn, fold firmly along the two lines. Fold up from the scored side. Turn the card over. Repeat for the lines on side B.

5 With the A side up, press the folds into the I-shape of the rail. Open out again. Glue the B side of the ¾in wide middle section as shown. Repeat for the second rail.

6 Give your two rails a metallic look by painting the upper (A) sides silver. Leave the paint to dry, and then apply a second coat. Leave the second coat to dry.

7 Use a pencil and ruler to mark ten 5 x ¾in strips on the foam board. Cut them out. Glue two strips together to make five thick railway sleepers. Leave them to dry.

8 Paint the sleepers brown on their tops and sides, to make them look like wood. Leave them to dry, then apply a second coat of paint. Leave the second coat to dry, too.

9 Lay the sleepers on the piece of paper, 1¼in apart. Make sure that they are exactly parallel to each other. Run a strip of masking tape down the middle to hold them in place.

10 Glue the base of a rail, and press into place with the outside edge of the rail ¾in in from the edge of the sleeper. Repeat with the other track. Secure with masking tape until it is dry.

Make several sets of rails. To join the rails together, roll up the thin card. Insert one end into the top of the I-shape. Push the second rail into the other end.

Rolling stock

The vehicle and machinery that is carried by a modern locomotive's underframe and wheels may weigh up to 100 tons. As bigger and more powerful locomotives were built, more wheels were added to carry the extra weight. Early steam locomotives had only two pairs of wheels. Later steam locomotives had two, three, or four pairs of driving wheels, one pair of which was directly driven from the cylinders. The cylinders house the pistons, whose movement pushes the driving wheels around via a connecting rod.

The other wheels are connected to the driving wheel by a coupling rod, so that they turn at the same time. The small wheels in front of the driving wheels are called leading wheels. The ones behind are the trailing wheels. Locomotives are defined by the total number of wheels they have. For example, a 4-4-0 type locomotive has four leading, four driving, and no trailing wheels. This project shows you how to make an underframe for a 4-4-0 type locomotive, which will run on the tracks described on the previous page. The following page shows how to make a locomotive to sit on the underframe.

▲ **Templates**

Draw and cut out the templates from the stiff card. Use a pair of compasses to draw the wheel templates A and B.

Make an underframe

1 Roll the rim templates C and D into rings. Glue and tape to hold. Glue each small wheel circle to each side of a small ring as shown. Repeat for big wheels. Leave to dry.

2 Use a pencil to enlarge the compass hole on one side of each wheel. Glue one end of each piece of dowel. Push them into the holes of two big and two small wheels.

3 Roll the 2 x 2in card into sleeves to fit loosely over each piece of dowel. Tape to hold. Make wheel pairs by fixing the remaining wheels to the dowel as described in step 2.

4 When the glue is dry, paint all four pairs of wheels silver. You do not need to paint the dowel axles. Paint two coats, letting the first dry before you apply the second.

5 Use a ruler and pencil to mark eight equal segments on the outside of each wheel. Paint a small circle over the compass hole, and the center of each segment black.

6 Fold along the dotted lines on E. Glue all three straight edges of template G and stick to template E. Repeat this for the other side. Secure all joints with masking tape.

7 Glue the open edges of the underframe. Fit template F on top and hold until firm. Tape over the joints. Give the underframe two coats of black paint. Leave to dry.

8 Glue the card sleeves to the base of the underframe. Small wheel axles go 1¼in and 2¾in from the front, big wheels 1¼in and 5in from the back. Tape to secure.

9 Paint the coupling rods (H) with a coat of silver paint. Allow the paint to dry thoroughly. Then give the coupling rods a second coat of paint, and leave them to dry.

10 Press a map pin through each end of the coupling rods, about ¼in from the edge. Carefully press the pin into each big wheel about ⅝in beneath the center.

The wheels of the underframe will fit on the model tracks just like those of a real train. In real trains, however, the wheels are mounted in swivelling units called "bogies."

Locomotive

Toy trains started to go on sale during the mid-1800s. Early models were made of brightly painted wood, and often had a wooden track to run along. Soon, metal trains went on sale, many of them made from tinplate (thin sheets of iron or steel coated with tin). Some of these metal toy trains had wind-up, clockwork motors. Clockwork toy trains were first sold in the USA during the 1880s. The most sophisticated model trains were steam-powered, with tiny engines fired by methyl alcohol burners. Later models were powered by electric motors.

Railroad companies often devised special color schemes, called liveries, for their locomotives and carriages. Steam locomotives had brass and copper decoration, and some also carried the company's logo or badge. Many toy trains are also painted in the livery of a real railroad company. The shape of the locomotive you can make in this project has an engine house that is typical of the real locomotives made in the 1930s. The driver and fireman would have shared the cabin of the locomotive. The driver controlled the speed of the train, and the fireman made sure there was a good supply of steam.

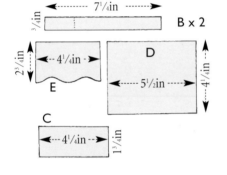

▲ **Templates**
Draw and cut out the templates from the stiff card.

Make a toy train

1 Roll the 10¼ x 10¼in card into an 3¼in diameter tube. Secure it with masking tape. Using the scissors, carefully cut a 2½in slit, 8½in from one end of the tube.

2 Hold the tube upright on the 4 x 4in piece of card. Draw around it. Cut this circle out. Glue the circle to the tube end farthest away from the slit. Tape to secure.

3 Copy and cut out the templates. Fold template A along the dotted lines. Fold templates B upward along the dotted line. Glue both strips to the cabin as shown, and secure with tape.

4 When the glue is dry, gently peel off the masking tape. Now glue on template C as shown above. Hold it in place with masking tape until the glue dries, and then remove the tape.

5 Apply two coats of green paint to the outside of the locomotive. Let the first coat dry before applying the second. Then paint the black parts. Add the red and gold last.

6 Glue around the bottom edge of the cabin front C. Put a little glue over the slit in the tube. Fit the front of the cabin into the slit. Leave the locomotive to one side to dry.

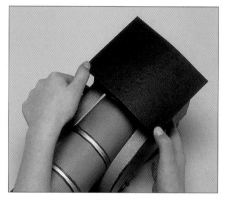

7 Give roof template D two coats of black paint. Let the paint dry between coats. Glue the top edges of the cabin, and place the black roof on top. Leave until dry and firm.

8 Glue the bottom of the cylindrical part of the train to the underframe you made in the "Underframe" project. Press thumb tacks into the back of cabin and underframe.

9 Glue both sides of one end of the red strip. Slot this between the underframe and the cabin, between the thumb tacks. When it is firm, fold the strip and insert the split pin.

10 Paint one side of template E black. When it is dry, roll it into a tube and secure with masking tape. Glue the wavy edge and secure it to the front of the locomotive as shown.

Just like a real locomotive, the basic color of your model train has been painted with red, black and gold decoration. The locomotive is now ready to run on the railway line you made in the "Making tracks" project on p206.

Brake van

Few early steam locomotives had brakes. If the driver needed to stop quickly, he had to throw the engine into reverse. By the early 1860s, braking systems for steam locomotives had been invented. Some passenger carriages also had their own handbrakes that were operated by the carriage guards. A brake van was added to the back of trains, too, but its brakes were operated by a guard riding inside. Old-style brake vans, like the one in this project, sat at the end of the train, so that the guard could make sure that all the carriages stayed coupled.

The problem was that the train driver had no control over the rest of the train. When he wanted to stop, he had to blow the engine whistle to warn each of the carriage guards to apply their brakes. The brakes on a locomotive and its carriages or wagons needed to be linked. This was made possible by the invention of an air-braking system in 1869. When the driver applies the brakes, compressed air travels along pipes that link all the train, and presses brake shoes. Air brakes are now used on nearly all the world's railroads.

YOU WILL NEED

large thick card, small piece of red card for template J, ruler, pencil, scissors, white glue and glue brush, masking tape, four 4in lengths of ¼in-diameter dowel, acrylic paints, paintbrush, water pot, two 1¼in lengths of ¼in-diameter dowel, compass.

▲ **Templates**

Make a brake van

1 Copy the templates onto card and cut them out. Glue templates A, B, and C together to make the underframe as shown. Tape over the joints to secure them.

2 Make and paint two pairs of small wheels (2in diameter) following steps 1 through 3 in the "Underframe" project on p208. Glue and tape the wheel pairs to the underframe.

3 Glue the bottom edges of the van sides (E) to the van base (D). Then glue on the van ends (F). Secure the joints with masking tape until the glue is dry.

4 Paint the brake van brown with black details, and the wheels and underframe black and silver. Apply two coats of paint, letting each one dry between coats.

5 Paint one side of template G black. Let the paint dry before applying a second coat. Glue the top edges of the van. Bend the roof to fit on the top of the van as shown.

6 Apply glue to the top surface of the underframe. Stick the brake van centrally on top. Press it together until the glue holds firm. Leave the model to dry completely.

7 Roll up templates I into two ¾in tubes to fit loosely over the 1¼in pieces of dowel. Tape to hold. Paint them silver. Paint the buffer templates H black and stick on each dowel.

8 Use a compass to pierce two holes 1in from each side of the van and ⅝in up. Enlarge with a pencil. Glue the end of each dowel buffer. Slot it into the hole. Leave to dry.

9 Cut a ¾in slot between the buffers. Fold the red card template J in half. Glue each open end of the loop, and push them through the slot. Press down to hold firm.

The brake van will also run on the tracks you made in the "Making tracks" project on p206. You can also join the red-card coupling to join the brake van to the model locomotive you made in the "Toy train" project on p210. On old-style railways, the brake van had one of two brake systems. One had hand-operated brakes that worked on the tread of the brake van's wheels. The other had a valve that allowed the guard to apply air brakes to all of the vehicles in the train.

Monorail

The first trains to run on a single rail rather than a twin track date back to the 1820s. As with early trains, these early monorails were pulled by horses and carried heavy materials, such as building bricks, rather than passengers. About 60 years later, engineers designed steam locomotives that hauled carriages along an A-shaped rail. However, neither the trains nor the carriages were very stable. Loads had to be carefully balanced on either side of the A-frame to stop them tipping over.

Today's monorails are completely stable, with several sets of rubber wheels to give a smooth ride. They are powered by electricity, and many are driverless. Driverless monorail trains are controlled by computers that tell them when to stop, start, speed up, or slow down. This project shows you how to make a train that runs on the "straddle" system monorail. The body of the train straddles over the rail.

Monorails are not widely used today, because they are more expensive to run than two-track railroads. The special track costs more to build than twin rails, and the cars cannot be switched from one track to another.

▲ Template
Draw and cut out the template from the stiff card.

Make a monorail

YOU WILL NEED

protective paper, 28in piece of wood (1½ x 1½in), acrylic paints, paintbrush, water pot, 26in length of plastic curtain rail (with screws, end fittings and four plastic runners), saw, screwdriver, sheet of stiff red card, pencil, ruler, scissors, double-sided tape, 7in piece of 1in-thick foam board, white glue and glue brush, black felt-tipped pen.

1 Cover the work surface with paper to protect it. Then paint the piece of wood yellow. Let the first coat dry thoroughly before applying a second coat of paint.

2 Ask an adult to saw the curtain rail to size if necessary. Place the track in the middle of the wood, and screw it into place. Screw in the end fittings at one end of the rail.

3 Copy the template onto the red card and cut it out. Score along the dotted lines and fold it inward. Stick double-sided tape along the outside of each folded section.

4 Remove the backing from the tape. Stick one side of the foam onto it. Fold the card over and press the other piece of double-sided tape to the opposite side of the foam.

5 Overlap the pointed ends at the back and front of the train and glue. Then glue the inside end of the top flaps, back and front. Fold them over and press firmly to secure.

6 Pencil in windows along both sides of the train. Fill them in with a black felt-tipped pen. Paint decorative yellow and black stripes along the bottom of the windows.

7 Put a dab of glue on the "eye" end of each plastic runner. Hold the train, foam bottom toward you. Push each runner into the foam at roughly equal intervals.

The train that you have made in this project is called a "straddle" system monorail. Monorail trains that run on the "straddle" system rest on a single rail and are balanced and guided by side panels on either side of the train.

8 Stand the track on a flat surface. At the end of the track without an end stop, feed each plastic runner into the track. Run the train back and forth along the track.

Making car wheels turn

cylinder head

spark plug

cylinder

piston

con
(connecting) rod

crankshaft

▲ Working together

Most car engines have four cylinders arranged like this. You can see the pistons and cylinders. Four rods, one from each piston, turn metal joints attached to the crankshaft. As the rods turn the joints, the crankshaft moves around. This movement is transmitted to the wheels, via the gearbox, which controls how fast the wheels turn relative to the engine.

This experiment shows how one kind of movement—that goes around and around—can be converted into an up-and-down movement. This idea is applied to cars to make the wheels go around, but it happens the other way around. The up-and-down movement of the pistons is changed into the circular motion of the crankshaft and wheels.

When a car engine is switched on, fuel ignites and hot gases are produced in the cylinders. The gases force close-fitting pistons down the cylinders in which they are housed. The pistons are connected to the crankshaft (a rod that connects eventually to the wheels), so that as they move up and down, the crankshaft rotates. This, in turn, makes the wheels go around. One up-and-down movement of a piston results in one turn of the crankshaft. The wheels rotate once for about every three to six turns of the crankshaft.

YOU WILL NEED

shoebox, thin metal rod about $\frac{1}{16}$in diameter, pliers, jelly jar lid, tape, scissors, thick plastic straw, ruler, pencil, stiff paper, at least four color felt-tipped pens, thin plastic straw.

Changing motion

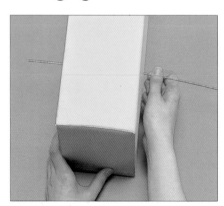

1 Place the shoebox narrow-side-down on a flat surface. With one hand, push the metal rod through the center, making sure that your other hand will not get jabbed by the rod.

2 Using the pliers, bend the rod at right angles where it comes out of the box. Attach the jelly jar lid to it with tape. Push the lid until it rests against the side of the box.

3 Carefully use the pliers to bend the piece of rod sticking out of the other side of the box. This will make a handle for the piston, so that you will be able to turn it easily.

4 Cut a piece of thick plastic straw about 2in long, and tape it to the side of the box close to the jelly jar lid. Make sure that it just sticks up beyond the edge of the box.

5 Draw a design in pencil on a piece of stiff paper. Copy the jester shown in this project, or draw a simple clown. Choose something that looks good when it moves.

6 Using the felt-tipped pens, color the design until it looks the way you want it to. The more colorful the figure is, the nicer it will look on the top of the piston.

7 Carefully cut the finished drawing out of the paper. Make sure that you have a clean-edged design. Try not to smudge the felt-tipped color with your fingers.

8 Turn the drawing over. Use the tape to attach the thin plastic straw to the bottom of the drawing. About ¾in of straw should be attached.

Place the box on end so the jester is at the top. Turn the handle on the front. As you turn the handle, the jelly jar lid revolves and pushes the jester up and down, like a piston.

9 Slide the straw attached to the drawing into the straw taped to the box. It will come out of the other end. Push down so that the straw touches the edge of the jelly jar lid.

Changing gear

Gears in a car help transfer movement in the most efficient way. They do this by transmitting movement from the crankshaft (which links engine and wheels) to another shaft called the propeller shaft. The propeller shaft rotates more slowly than the crankshaft and adapts the movement, so that the car can cope better with different speeds and efforts, such as starting and going uphill. The change in speed of rotation between the two shafts is controlled from the car's gearbox. As a driver changes gear, toothed wheels that are connected to the crankshaft engage with other toothed wheels joined to the propeller shaft. The difference in the number of teeth on each wheel determines the number of times the wheels turn, as the first project demonstrates. The second experiment shows how gear wheels work in a car. The larger corrugated card wheel has more teeth than the two smaller wheels.

crankshaft

propeller shaft

high gear

low gear

▲ Wheels within wheels

The car's engine turns the crankshaft with different-sized gears (toothed wheels) on it. High gears are used for more speed, because the big wheel turns the small wheel faster. The gear system is called the transmission—it transmits (moves) the engine's power to the car's wheels. Most cars have five gears. The biggest is needed for slow speeds, and the smallest for high speeds.

YOU WILL NEED

compass, ruler, pencil, 8½ x 11in sheet of white paper, black pen, scissors, 8½ x 11in sheet of thin card, two strips of corrugated card, tape, three colored felt-tipped pens.

Drawing the gears

1 Using the compass, trace a 5½in-diameter circle on the paper. Draw over it with the pen and cut it out. On the card, trace, draw, and cut out an 4¼in-diameter circle.

2 Tape corrugated card around the circles. Make a hole in the small circle wide enough for the tip of a felt-tipped pen. Turn the small wheel inside the larger. Trace the path in felt-tipped pen.

3 Make a second hole in the small wheel. Turn the small gear inside the larger using another felt-tipped pen. Make a third hole in the small wheel and use a third color pen.

Three-gear machine

YOU WILL NEED

compass, ruler, pencil,

8½ x 11in sheet of card, pen, scissors,

three strips of corrugated card,

tape, 8½ x 11in piece of fiberboard,

white glue, 2½in piece of

⅝in-diameter wood dowel,

three map pins.

1 Use the compass to trace one 5½in-diameter and two 4¼in-diameter circles on the card. Draw around the circle edges with the pen, and cut the circles out.

2 Carefully wrap the strips of corrugated card around the circles, using one strip per circle, corrugated side out. Tape each strip to the bottom of the circles.

3 Place the largest gear wheel on the piece of fiberboard. Hold the gear down and glue the dowel on to the side of the gear base at the edge of the wheel. Leave it until it is dry.

4 Position all three gears on the fiberboard, with the edges just touching each other. Pin each of them firmly to the fiberboard with a map pin, but allow them to turn.

As you turn the gears, notice how they move in opposite directions to each other. Now you have a three-gear machine, where the energy from each gear is being transferred to the others, just like the gears in a car.

5 Gently turn the dowel on the largest gear. As that gear turns, the two others that are linked together by the corrugated card will turn against it.

Car control

Cars have two kinds of brakes. Parking brakes lock the rear wheels when the car is standing still. Disk brakes slow down the car when it is moving, in the same way that the sandpaper slows the model wheel in the first experiment.

The second project shows how a device called the camshaft controls the flow of fuel into the cylinders. The camshaft is designed so as to have a regular action that opens one valve and closes another at the same time. Inlet valves let fuel and air into the engine, and burned waste gases are removed via the outlet valves. The camshaft controls make the engine run smoothly.

filtered air

gasoline

fuel and air mixture

▲ The carburetor

Fuel and air enter the carburetor in just the right quantities for the car to run smoothly. The mixture is then fed into the cylinders. Pressing the accelerator pedal in a car allows more air and fuel into the engine to make it run faster, so speeding up the car.

Stopping ▶

When a driver presses the brake pedal, a piston presses together two pads, one on either side of the disk to which the wheel is attached. This strong grip stops the disk from turning, and as the disk slows, so do the wheels.

piston

disk

wheel attached here

calliper

brake pads

YOU WILL NEED

Disk brakes: scissors, 16in piece of fabric, circular card box with lid, tape, pencil, 8in piece of ⅝in-diameter wood dowel, white glue, glue brush, 2¾ x 4¼in medium sandpaper, 2½ x 4in wooden block, two plastic cups, insulation tape.

How valves work: scissors, 4½in square of stiff card, masking tape, cardboard tube with plastic lid, pencil.

Disk brakes

1 Use the scissors to cut a narrow 16in strip from the fabric. You may have to use special fabric cutting scissors if your ordinary scissors are not sharp enough.

2 Take the strip of fabric you have cut out, and wrap it around the rim of the circular cardboard box. Secure it firmly in place with small pieces of tape.

3 Make a hole in the center of the box's lid with a pencil. Twist the pencil until it comes through the base of the box. Now gently push the wood dowel through both holes.

4 Spread lots of glue onto the sandpaper's smooth side. Wrap the sandpaper carefully over the top of the wood block. Pressing firmly, stick it together. Leave it to dry.

5 Stand two plastic cups upside down. Rest either end of the dowel on each cup. Cut two small pieces of insulation tape. Use them to fix each end of the dowel to the cup bases.

6 Spin the lid fast on the dowel. As it spins, bring the sandpaper into contact with the edge of the lid. Test your brake disk to see how quickly you can stop the lid.

How valves work

1 Use scissors to cut a ½ x 4½in strip from the stiff card. Double it over in the center. Hold it with your fingertips. Bend the two ends of the card away from one another.

2 Cut a ½ x 1½in strip from the original piece of card. Use masking tape to fix the card strip to the bent bottom ends of the first piece. This makes a triangle shape.

3 Use the scissors to cut out two small circle shapes from the original piece of card. Use masking tape to secure them to the bottom piece of the triangle you have made.

4 Put the stiff card triangle on top of the cardboard tube. The circles should touch the plastic lid. With a pencil, mark the position where the circles sit on the lid.

5 Using the scissors, carefully cut around the pencil marks you have made in the plastic lid of the tube. These form an inlet and an outlet. As one valve opens, the other will close.

6 Now you can rock the triangle back and forth, to cover and uncover the two holes. This is just how a camshaft opens and shuts the inlet and outlet valves in a car's cylinder.

Keeping cool

The explosion of fuel and air that fires a car's engine generates a great deal of heat. Friction (rubbing together of two surfaces), as the engine parts move together at speed, also creates heat. If the heat level is not kept down, the engine stops working. Metal parts expand, seize up, and stop. To cool the engine, water from the car's radiator is pumped around the hottest parts of the engine—the combustion chambers, where the fuel ignites, and the cylinders.

▲ **Mass production**

All the separate parts of a car are mass-produced and then assembled (put together) on a production line to make the finished vehicle. Almost all cars are assembled on production lines today. Robots do much of the work.

The moving water carries heat away from the hottest parts of the engine. The radiator cools the hot water from the engine by using a fan. The fan is driven by a belt connected to the engine. This project shows how a belt transfers turning movement from one shaft to another. This is how a car's engine turns the fan belt.

```
YOU WILL NEED

ruler, 6¼in square of thin cloth,
scissors, five reels of thread, glue stick,
8½ x 11in wooden board, pencil, five
flat-headed nails 1½in long, hammer,
1yd x 1in velvet ribbon, tape, compass,
five pieces of 4in-square colored card,
five wooden skewers.
```

Fan belt

1 Using the ruler, measure five 1in-wide strips on the thin cloth. The height of the reels of thread should be more than 1in. Use the scissors to cut out each strip.

2 Wrap one of the fabric strips around each of the five reels of thread. Glue each strip at the end, so that it sits firmly around the reel and will not come loose.

3 Place the reels on the wooden board as shown above. Trace the outlines with a pencil. Put the nails through the center of the reels, and carefully hammer them into the board.

4 Wind the ribbon around the reels, with the velvet side against four of the reels. Cut the ribbon at the point where you can join both ends around the fifth reel.

5 Tape the two ends of the ribbon together firmly. Make sure that the ribbon wraps firmly around all of the five reels, but not so tightly that it can't move.

6 Use the compass to draw circles about ¾in in diameter onto the five pieces of colored card. Then carefully draw freehand spiral shapes inside each circle.

7 Use the scissors to cut each spiral out of each of the pieces of coloured card. Start from the outside edge, and gradually work your way in along the lines of the spiral.

8 Tape one end of each spiral to the end of a skewer. Wind the other end of the spiral around the skewer stick a few times. Tape it close to the opposite end of the skewer.

Now you are ready to turn the belt. Like a fan belt in a car, it turns the fans around. This is a five-fan machine. You can add more fans if you like.

9 Put a small amount of tape onto the end of each wooden skewer. Then place each skewer into one of the empty holes in the top of each reel of thread.

Prototype car

When you make your model car, choose the colors carefully. Do you want bright colors that will be noticed easily, or cool, fashionable colors? Car manufacturers call in teams of people to help them decide what a car should look like. Stylists, and design and production engineers join forces with the sales team to develop cars they hope people will buy. They think about the colors, how much people are prepared to pay, and what features they want, from air-conditioning to special car seats.

Before a new car is launched to the public, detailed models are made and tested to investigate the car's aerodynamics (how air flows over its shape). Finally, a prototype (early version) of the car is built and tested for road handling, engine quality, and comfort.

YOU WILL NEED

Model car: two 8½ x 11in sheets of card, compass, ruler, pencil, scissors, white glue, glue brush, bradawl, 6in square piece of colored card, pliers, four paper clips, two 4in lengths of ⅝in-diameter wood dowel, tape.

Decorate your car: two colors of acrylic paints, medium paintbrushes, pencil, two pieces of 6 x 8in colored card, a piece of white card, two colors of felt-tipped pens, scissors, white glue.

Wire basket ▶

Car designers today make use of CAD (computer-aided design) software to help them create a three-dimensional image of a new car design. Wire-frame (see-through) computer images show the car from any angle. They also show how all the parts of the car fit together.

Model car

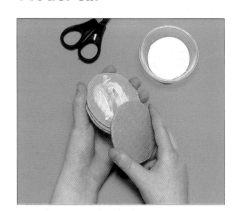

1 Draw and cut out four 1in and eight 2½in diameter card circles. Glue the 2½in circles together to make four wheels. Glue a 1in circle to the center of each wheel.

2 Use the bradawl to make a hole in the center of each wheel. Cut four ⅛in strips of colored card. Wrap one each around the wheel rims. Glue the overlapping ends.

3 Push straightened paper clips into the holes, and bend the outer ends with pliers. Fix the wheels to the two pieces of dowel by pushing the paper clips into the ends.

4 Cut a piece of card to 2¾ x 6in. Trim one end to make it 2½in wide. Tape the two axles to the card, one at each end. Make sure they are long enough for the wheels to rotate freely.

5 Cut a piece of card 3¼ x 14in. Double it over and bend it into a British cab shape. Tape the two loose ends together. Stick the base of the cab shape to the car base.

6 Cut two cardboard shapes 6in long and 4in high. Trim them with the scissors to the same shape as the side of your car cab. Attach the sides to the cab with tape.

Decorate your car

Replace the wheels when they are dry. Now your car looks just like a real vehicle. Cut photographs of cars from magazines to get ideas for new designs.

1 Remove the wheels from your car. Paint the sides and top of the cab with one of the two colors of paint. Leave it to dry. Then paint it with the same color again, and leave it to dry.

2 Draw exciting designs for the sides of the car and a driver to go behind the windscreen. Draw some head lamps and some exhaust fumes. Add color with the felt-tipped pens.

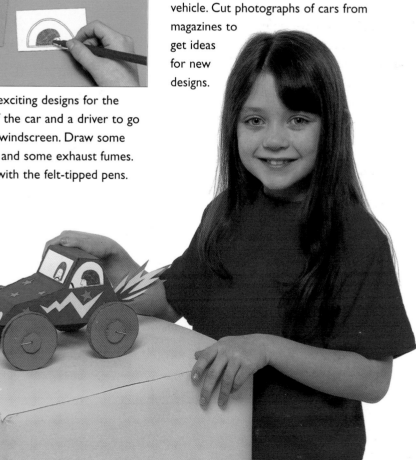

3 Let the paint dry for a couple of hours. Cut the designs out of the card. Glue them to the sides and back of the car. Paint the wheels with the color of paint you haven't used.

Parachutes and balloons

Parachutes fall slowly because air is trapped beneath them. They are deliberately designed to have very high drag. Drag is the force that works against the direction of anything that flies through the air. The amount of drag depends on the shape. A fat, lumpy shape, like the parachute in the first project, has lots of drag and falls slowly.

Hot air balloons rise into the air, because the hot air inside them is lighter than the air outside. Real balloons use gas burners, but the project here uses a hair dryer to make the balloon rise.

YOU WILL NEED

felt-tipped pen, a large plate, thin fabric, scissors, needle, thread, tape, plastic thread reel.

Mini-parachute jump

1 Use the felt-tipped pen to draw around the plate on the fabric. Using the scissors, carefully cut out the circle to make what will be the parachute's canopy.

2 Make about eight equally spaced marks around the edge of the circle. Use a needle to sew on one 12in long piece of thread to each point you have marked.

3 Use tape to secure the free end of each thread to a reel. Use a plastic reel, because a wooden one will be too heavy for your parachute.

4 Hold the parachute so that the canopy is open and the thread reel dangles down. Stand by an upstairs window, or use a step-ladder to get as high as you can—but be very careful!

Let your parachute go from as high up as possible. As it falls, the canopy will open and fill with air. The larger the canopy, the slower the parachute will fall.

Ballooning around

1 To make a template, draw a petal shape on card and carefully cut it out. The shape should be 12in long and 4½in across with a flat bottom edge.

2 Draw around your template on seven pieces of colored tissue paper. Be very careful not to rip the tissue paper with the tip of your pencil.

3 Use the pair of scissors to carefully cut out the shapes you have drawn. You should now have seven petals that are all the same size and shape.

To fly your balloon, hold its neck open and fill the inside with hot air from a hair dryer. After ten seconds, switch off the hair dryer and let go of your balloon to launch it into the air.

4 Glue along one edge of a petal. Lay another petal on top, and press it down. Open it out and stick on another petal in the same way. Keep going until the balloon is complete.

Streamlined design

Think of a sleek canoe moving through the water. Its streamlined shape hardly makes any ripples as it passes. Streamlined shapes also move easily through the air. They have low drag (air resistance). Angular shapes have more drag than rounded ones. The shape of a fast-moving fish has to be very streamlined. A fish such as a tuna has a blunt front end, is broadest about a third of the way along, then tapers towards the tail. This creates less drag as it moves through water than a shape with a pointed front end that broadens at the back. Water flows along each side of the tuna to rejoin without creating turbulence. The "Shape race" gives you a chance to design and test your own streamlined shapes.

Just as things that are moving in the air experience drag, so do stationary objects in the wind. Kites, such as the one here, are held up in the air by drag from the wind. For more than 3,000 years, people have been making and flying kites. The essential, but simple, secret is that it must be as light as possible for its size, so that it catches as much wind as possible. The kite design shown in this project has been used for many hundreds of years. Try flying it first of all in a steady wind, and experiment with the position of the bridle and the length of the tail.

YOU WILL NEED

pen, ruler, two bamboo canes (one about two-thirds as long as the other), string, scissors, tape, sheet of thin fabric or plastic, fabric glue, colored paper.

▲ **How air flows work**
Air flows in gentle curves around the streamlined shape (*top*). Angles and sharp curves break up the flow and increase drag (*bottom*).

star

teardrop

square

▲ **Shape race**
Make different shapes (as shown above) from balls of modeling material that are exactly the same size. Race your shapes in water—the most streamlined shape should reach the bottom first.

Make a kite

1 To make the frame, mark the center of the short cane and mark one-third of the way up the long cane. Tie the canes together crosswise at the marks with string.

2 Tape string around the ends of the canes and secure it at the top. This will stop the canes from moving, and it will also support the edges of your finished kite.

3 Lay the frame on top of the sheet of fabric or plastic. Cut around it, ¾in away from the kite's edge. This will give you enough to fold over the string outline.

4 Fold each edge of the material over the frame, and stick the edges down firmly with fabric glue (or tape if you are making the kite from plastic). Let the glue dry.

5 Tie a piece of string to the long cane, as shown—this is called the bridle. Tie the end of the ball of string to the middle of the bridle to make the tether.

6 Fold sheets of paper in zigzags. Tie them at about 10in intervals along a piece of string that is about twice as long as the kite. Glue or tie the tail to the bottom tip of the kite.

bridle

tail

tassel

tether

Now your kite is ready to fly! With the wind blowing on your back, reel out about 10yds of tether. Ask an adult to gently launch the kite into the air. If it is not very windy, run into the breeze, pulling the kite to get it airborne. Now that you have built this kite, try experimenting with other materials and shapes, to find out which ones work well.

Curve and lift

Birds, gliders, and airplanes all have wings. Their wings can be all sorts of different shapes and sizes, but they all have the same airfoil design. This means that the top side of the wing is more curved than the underside. The airfoil shape provides lift when air moves over it. Air flows faster over the curved upper surface than over the flatter lower surface. This reduces the air pressure above the wing, and lets the higher air pressure underneath lift it up.

You can make and test a model airfoil by following the instructions in these projects. In the frisbee project, the shape of the frisbee allows the air to move smoothly over and under it. The frisbee spins as it flies. The spinning motion helps to steady it. The second project shows you how moving air, in this case, from an electric fan or hair dryer, can lift the wings with an airfoil shape upward.

Fly a frisbee

1 Place the plate face down on the card, and draw around it with a pencil. Cut out the circle of card. Draw slots ¾ in deep around the edge and cut these, as shown.

2 The cut slots around the edge will make tabs. Bend the tabs down slightly. Overlap them a little and stick them together with small pieces of tape.

Fly your frisbee outside, away from people. Hold it at the front and spin it away from you and up. It should glide through the air smoothly as the air pressure above it is reduced. Play toss-and-catch games with your friends. You could even have your own championship match! Commercial frisbees were introduced into the USA in the 1950s.

Aerofoil antics

1 Use a ruler to measure a rectangle of colored paper about 6in wide and 8in long. Use scissors to carefully cut out the shape. This will be your wing.

2 Fold the paper over, approximately in half. Use tape to fix the top edge ½in away from the bottom edge. Take care not to crease the paper as you do this.

3 Cut out and stick on a small paper fin near the rear edge of your wing, as shown. This will keep the wing facing into the airflow when you test it.

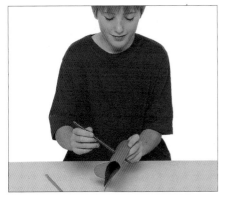

4 With a sharp pencil, carefully poke a hole through the top and bottom of your wing, near the front edge. Push a straw through the holes and glue it in place in the middle.

5 Cut a 1yd-long piece of thick thread and thread it through the straw. Make sure that the thread can slide easily through the straw and does not catch.

Hold the thread tight, and ask a friend to blow air from a fan or hair dryer over the wing. Watch it take off! This happens because the shape decreases the air pressure above the wing.

Jet propulsion

A jet engine produces thrust from a roaring jet of super-hot gas. Its construction looks complicated, but the way it works is very simple. A powerful jet of gas moving in one direction produces thrust in the other direction. Imagine you are standing on a skateboard and squirting a powerful hose forward. Jet propulsion will push you backward. This reaction has been known for nearly 2,000 years, but it was not until the 1930s that it was applied to an engine.

In the first experiment, you can make a jet zoom along a string. The jet engine is like a balloon that produces thrust from escaping air. The second project demonstrates how a turbine works. Hot air produced by the gas jet turns the blades of the turbine. The turbine drives the fan at the front of the jet engine. These projects may seem simple, but they use the same scientific principles that propel all jet airplanes through the air.

YOU WILL NEED

Balloon jet: long, thin balloon, scissors, tape, drinking straw, string.

Turbine lights: aluminum pie tin, scissors, compass, protractor, ruler, pin, 3in length of ⅛in dowel, tape, bead, thread reel, nonhardening modeling material, plate, four night light candles, matches.

Balloon jet

I Blow up the balloon and, while a friend holds the neck, tape the straw to its top. Thread the string through the straw and, holding it level, tie it to something to keep it in place.

▲ **Practical plane**
This passenger plane has four engines, two on each wing. Jet engines have revolutionized international travel. Passenger planes carry millions of travelers around the world every year.

2 Let go of the neck of the balloon. A stream of air jets backward and produces thrust. This propels the balloon forward along the string at high speed.

2 Decorate your bottle to look like a rocket. Fold the tab at the top of each fin. Use long pieces of strong tape to attach the fins to the bottle firmly.

3 Use the funnel to half-fill the bottle with water. (The water is the propellant. Compressed air above the water will provide the energy that makes the thrust.)

4 Use the bradawl to drill a hole carefully through the cork. Push the wide end of the air valve into the plastic tube. Push the valve through the hole in the cork.

5 Hold the bottle with one hand, and push the cork and the valve into the neck of the bottle using the other hand. Push it in firmly so that the cork does not slide out too easily.

6 Attach the other end of the plastic tube to the bicycle pump. Turn your rocket the right way up—you are now ready to launch your rocket outside.

Look for a launch site far away from trees and buildings. Stand the rocket on its tail fins, and tell everyone to stand well back. Start pumping. Bubbles of air will rise up through the water. When the pressure in the bottle gets high enough, the cork and the water will be forced out and the rocket will fly upward. Be careful not to stand over the bottle!

Going to the Moon

Plotting a course through Space is more complicated than traveling over land. Pilots follow natural features, such as hills, valleys, and rivers; at high altitudes, they use radio beacons on the ground or satellite signals. The problem with traveling from the Earth to the Moon is that both are moving, as the first project illustrates. The second project shows how a heavy craft gets to the Moon. Staged rockets release their sections as they progress into Space, so reducing the weight of the rocket.

If a spacecraft was aimed straight at the Moon when it set off from Earth, the Moon would have moved on around its orbit by the time the craft arrived. If the spacecraft corrected its direction to follow the Moon's orbit, it would use too much fuel. Spacecraft are therefore aimed at the position the Moon will be in by the time the craft arrives. They navigate by the stars.

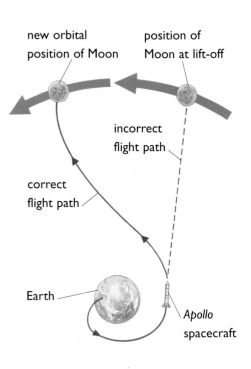

▲ **Moving targets**

This diagram shows two possible flight paths for an *Apollo* spacecraft. Aiming directly at the Moon does not allow for its movement as it orbits the Earth. The correct, efficient route compensates for the Moon's orbital movements by aiming ahead of its position at lift-off.

YOU WILL NEED

Moving target: string, ruler, scissors, masking tape, metal washer, book, small balls of paper.

Two-stage rocket: two paper or plastic cups, scissors, long balloon and pump, tape, round balloon.

Moving target

1 Measure 2ft of string with the ruler. Cut it off with scissors. Tape one end of the string to one end of the ruler. Tie a washer to the other end of the string.

2 Place the ruler on a table or box, with the string hanging over the edge. Weigh it down with a heavy book. Try hitting the washer by throwing small balls of paper at it.

3 Start the washer swinging, and try to hit it again with the paper balls. See how much more difficult it is to hit a moving target, like a spacecraft aiming at the moving Moon.

third stage powers command/service module (CSM) toward the Moon

third stage fires

second stage fires

second stage jettisoned

first stage jettisoned

▲ Rocket staging

The *Saturn 5* rocket had three stages. The first two powered the spacecraft up through the atmosphere. The third stage propelled it into orbit, and then gave an extra push to send the craft on its way to the Moon.

Two-stage rocket

I Using scissors, carefully cut the bottoms out of the paper or plastic cups. These will serve as the linking collar between the two stages of the balloon rocket.

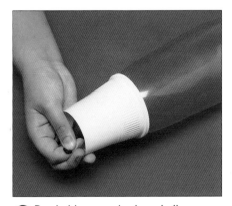

2 Partly blow up the long balloon with the pump. Pull the neck of the balloon through the paper or plastic cups. This balloon will be your two-stage rocket's second stage.

3 Fold the neck of the long balloon over the side of the cups. Tape the end of the neck of the balloon to the cups to stop the air from escaping, as shown.

4 Carefully push the round balloon into the open end of the paper or plastic cups, as shown. This balloon will form the first stage of your two-stage balloon rocket.

5 Blow up the round balloon, so that it wedges the neck of the long balloon in place inside the cups. Hold the neck of the round balloon to keep the air inside it.

Peel the tape off the neck of the long balloon. Hold the rocket as shown. Let go of the round balloon's neck. Air rushes out, launching the first stage of the rocket. It then falls away, launching the second-stage balloon.

Artificial gravity

Space travelers in orbit far away from Earth do not feel the pull of gravity. They feel weightless, as if they are forever falling. In a state of weightlessness, there is no up or down, because up and down are created by the force known as gravity. Even experienced pilots and astronauts sometimes feel uncomfortable and ill until they get used to being weightless. Weightlessness also has damaging effects on the human body. Future space stations and spacecraft designed for very long spaceflights may create artificial gravity to protect their occupants from the effects of weightlessness.

Make a centrifuge

In this project, you can explore a theoretical method of creating artificial gravity that uses rotation by making a centrifuge. Moving objects tend to travel in straight lines. When you whirl around a ball attached to the end of a piece of string, it tries to fly off in a straight line, stopped only by the string. Inside a rotating spacecraft, the solid outer walls would stop astronauts flying off in straight lines. This would feel like the astronauts were being pushed down to the ground, just like the effect of gravity on Earth.

1 Take the four card triangles and tape them to the sides of the bottle, as shown. These will provide the dishwashing detergent centrifuge with a broad, stable base to stand on.

2 Using the bradawl, make a hole in the bottom of the detergent bottle. Push one end of the rubber band almost all the way into the hole using a wooden skewer.

3 Pass the wooden skewer through the small loop of rubber band projecting from the hole, as shown. Leave an equal amount of skewer on either side of the bottle.

4 Take the masking tape and firmly secure the wooden skewer to the base of the detergent bottle. Make sure that the skewer is fixed so tightly that it cannot move.

5 Straighten out one end of a paper clip with pliers. Dip the hooked end of the clip into the neck of the bottle. Catch the rubber band with the hook and pull it out.

6 Using the bradawl, make a hole in the middle of the 20 x 2in card strip. Thread the end of the hooked paper clip through the bead. Then thread it through the hole in the card.

7 Carefully bend the end of the paper clip down onto the card strip. Using the tape, fix the end of the clip securely into place, as shown above.

8 Use the scissors to cut two short pieces of drinking straw. Each piece should measure 2in in length. Fix one piece to each end of the card strip with the tape.

9 Take one of the small plastic cups. Carefully make a hole with the scissors on both sides of the cup near the top. Now make holes in the second cup in the same way.

Stick the centrifuge to a flat surface with modeling material. Fill the cups one-quarter full with water. Add food coloring to make the water show up clearly. Then turn the card strip until the rubber band is wound up. Let the strip go, and watch the cups as they spin around rapidly. The cups fly outward, but the water is held in place by bases of the cups.

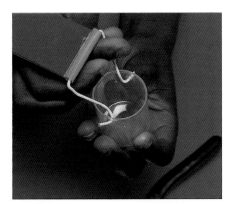

10 Straighten two paper clips with pliers. Thread a clip through each straw. Bend the ends of the clips into hooks using pliers. Thread the ends of the clips through the holes in the cups.

Working in Space

▲ Working in a spacesuit

Bulky spacesuits make working in space difficult. Spacesuit designers are always trying to improve them. The more flexible a suit is, the less tiring it is to work in. This means that an astronaut can work outside for longer periods, a great help when they are making repairs.

There is no gravity outside the pressurized crew compartment of a shuttle in Space. This makes work more difficult than on Earth. On Earth, gravity pulls us down to the ground. We can then use friction against the ground in order to move around. If a weightless astronaut pushes a handle in zero gravity, he or she would fly away in the opposite direction! This means that astronauts have to be anchored to something solid before doing any work. A spacesuit makes it even more difficult to move. The astronaut has to push against the suit to close a hand, or bend an arm or leg.

Spacesuit gloves have thin rubber fingerpacks, so that astronauts can feel things through them, but their sense of touch is still very limited. The first

project simulates the experience of working in a spacesuit by using rubber gloves, a bowl of water, and some nuts and bolts. Then make a robot arm like the shuttle's remote manipulator system (RMS), which is used to launch and retrieve satellites.

Working in Space

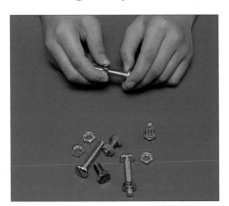

1 Take the nuts and bolts, and place them on a table. Now try picking them up and screwing them together. You should find this a very easy task to achieve!

2 Now try screwing the nuts and bolts together with the gloves on. This is more difficult, like trying to perform a delicate task on Earth wearing bulky spacesuit gloves.

3 Fill the bowl with water. Add the nuts and bolts. Try screwing them together with the gloves on. This is very difficult, like working in a spacesuit outside a spacecraft.

Make a robot arm

1 Use the ruler to measure three 11 x 2in card strips. Cut them out. Use a bradawl to make a hole 1in from the ends of each strip. Join the strips with split pins.

2 Take the hook and screw it into the end of the dowel. The dowel will be used to control the robot arm remotely, just as shuttle astronauts remotely operate the RMS.

3 Now carefully bend one of the paper clips into the shape of the letter S. To attach the paper clip, pass it through the hole in the end of the cardboard arm, as shown.

4 Take the modeling material and roll it into a ball about the size of a walnut. Then take the second paper clip and push it firmly into the ball, as shown.

Pass the hook on the dowel through the hole in the end of the cardboard arm. Move the dowel to operate the robot arm remotely. Try to pick up the ball using the S-shaped paper clip.

Glossary

A

aerodynamics The way in which objects move through the air.

aileron A moving flap on the trailing (rear) edge of an aircraft wing.

air pressure The force with which air presses on things. Changes in air pressure makes air move, and causes different weather conditions.

airfoil An object, shaped like a wing, that creates lift in the air.

alloy A material, usually a metal, such as bronze or brass, that is made from a mixture of other materials.

aperture A hole behind the lens of a camera, which can be adjusted to let more or less light on to the film.

APS (Advanced Photographic System) A camera that allows you to change the format for individual shots.

artificial Describes something that is not created as part of a natural process or with naturally occuring materials.

atmosphere The layer of air that surrounds a planet and is held to it by the planet's gravity.

atom The smallest part of an element that can exist. It is made up of many other smaller particles including electrons, neutrons, and protons.

autofocus A feature on a camera that automatically adjusts the lens position to make sure that a scene is in focus.

B

bacteria A simple living organism, usually consisting of a single cell. Many bacteria are parasites and cause disease.

battery A container of chemicals that holds a charge of electricity.

binary code The digital code computers use, made up of two numbers, "0" and "1".

bow The front end of a ship.

brake A pad or disk that slows a moving surface down by pressing it.

brake van A carriage at the back of trains used in the mid-1800s. A guard riding in the brake van applied the brakes following instructions from the driver in the locomotive.

C

CAD Computer-aided design.

camouflage The adoption of colors, patterns, and texture in order to merge with the environment and so be hidden or disguised.

camshaft A device that creates a regular, rocking movement, such as the opening and shutting of a valve on a car cylinder head.

carbon dioxide A colorless, odorless gas containing the elements carbon and oxygen, which is a part of air.

cargo Goods carried in a ship or other vehicle.

caterpillar The larva of a butterfly or moth.

CD-ROM (compact disk read-only memory) A portable computer disk, similar to an audio CD, that stores information.

chemical A substance used by scientists, in industry and at home.

chemical reaction The process by which one or more substances react together and change into one or more different chemicals.

chlorophyll The green pigment of plants that absorbs light energy from the Sun.

climate The typical weather pattern of an area.

cocoon A silky, protective envelope, such as that secreted by silkworms and other insect larvae, to protect the developing pupa.

compass An instrument that contains a magnetized strip of metal, used for finding direction.

compressed air Air that has been squashed into a smaller volume than usual.

condensation The process by which water vapor becomes a liquid.

conductor A material through which heat or electricity can travel.

continental drift The generally accepted theory that continents move slowly around the world.

continental shelf The zone of shallow water in the oceans around the edge of continents.

convection The rising of hot air or fluid, caused by the fact that it is lighter than its surroundings.

counterweight A weight that balances another weight.

coupling A connecting device that joins a locomotive to a carriage to make a train.

coupling rod A link that connects the driving wheels on both sides of a locomotive.

crankshaft An axle that has parts of it bent at right angles so that up-and-down motion can be turned into circular motion.

crystal A mineral or other substance that forms in a regular, 3-dimensional shape.

cylinder A hollow or solid tube shape.

D

data Pieces of information.

database An organized store of information.

deciduous Describes trees and shrubs that shed their leaves at the end of each growing season.

density A measure of how tightly the matter in a substance is packed together.

deposition The laying down of material, particularly of material eroded from the Earth's crust and carried by rivers, sea, and ice.

depth of field In photography, the

distance in focus between the nearest and farthest parts of a scene.

digital camera A camera that takes electronic images that are downloaded onto a computer to be viewed.

dish antenna A large, dish-shaped aerial used to receive signals in radar, radio telescopes, and satellite broadcasting.

disk drive The device that holds, reads, and writes on to a disk.

drag A force that acts in the opposite direction to motion and creates resistance.

driving wheel The wheel of a locomotive that turns in response to power from the steam engine.

E

Earth's crust The outermost, solid rock layer of the planet Earth.

ecosystem A community of living things that interact with each other and their surroundings.

effort The force applied to a lever or other simple machine to move a load.

electricity A form of energy caused by the movement of electrons (charged particles) in atoms.

element A substance that cannot be split by chemical processes into simpler parts.

elevator In aircraft, a movable flap on the tailplane or rear wing that causes the nose to rise and fall.

engine A device that uses energy in fuel to make movement.

environment The external conditions in which people, animals, and plants live on Earth.

epicentre The region on the Earth's surface that lies directly above the focus of an earthquake.

Equator The imaginary circle around the middle of the Earth, between the Northern and Southern Hemispheres,

where day and night are equal in length, and the climate is constantly hot and wet.

erosion The gradual wearing away of the land by agents of erosion such as ice, rain, wind, and waves.

escape velocity The minimum speed that a body must have to escape from the gravitational force of a planet.

evaporation The process by which something turns from liquid to vapor.

evergreen Describes plants that bear leaves all the year round.

exoskeleton Outer skeleton—the hard case that protects an insect's soft body parts.

exposure time The time it takes for a camera to take a picture.

exposures Photographs on a film.

F

fault A break in the Earth's crust that causes one block of rock to slip against an adjacent one.

fax machine A machine that photocopies and electronically sends and receives written words and pictures over a telephone line.

fertilization The act or process of the male part of a plant, or a male animal, that allows a female's seed, egg or eggs to produce young.

focal plane The area at the back of a camera where the exposed film is held flat.

force A push or a pull.

fossil The remains, found preserved in rock, of a creature that lived in the past.

freight Goods transported by rail, road, sea, and air.

friction The force caused by the two surfaces rubbing together. This results in the slowing down of movement and heat being produced.

fumarole An opening in the ground in volcanic regions, where steam and gases can escape.

G

gauge The width between the inside running edges of the rails of a train track. In Britain, the USA and most of Europe, the gauge is 56½in.(1,435mm).

gear A toothed wheel designed to interact with other toothed wheels to transfer motion in a controlled way.

generate To produce energy such as electricity.

geology The scientific study of the origins and structure of a planet and its rocks.

geothermal energy The energy created by the heat of the rocks underground.

germination The point at which a plant seed, or an egg in an animal, is fertilized and begins to grow.

geyser A fountain of steam and water that spurts out of a vent in the ground in volcanic regions.

gravity The pulling force that exists between large masses.

H

hard disk A computer's main storage disk, which holds the operating system and application files.

hardware All the equipment that makes up a computer—disk drives, monitor, keyboard, mouse, etc.

hemispheres The top and bottom halves of the Earth, divided by the Equator, and known as the Northern and Southern Hemispheres.

hibernation A period when many animals save energy by remaining inactive in order to survive the winter.

hot spot A place where plumes of molten rock in the Earth's mantle burn through the Earth's crust to create isolated areas of volcanic activity.

hot springs Water that has been heated underground and bubbles to the surface in volcanic regions.

hull The frame or body of a ship or aircraft.

humidity The amount of water, or moisture, in the air.

hydraulics The use of water and other liquids to move devices such as pistons.

hydrometer An instrument for measuring the density of liquids.

hygrometer An instrument for measuring humidity.

I

igneous rock A rock that forms when magma (hot, molten rock) cools and becomes solid. One of three main types of rock, created as hot molten rock from the Earth's interior, cools and solidifies.

infrared Electromagnetic radiation with a wavelength between the red end of the visible spectrum, and microwaves and radio waves.

insulate To cover or protect something to reduce the amount of heat or electricity entering and/or leaving it.

J

jet engine a type of engine that propels a vehicle, such as a car or a plane, by the forceful expulsion of hot gases.

jet propulsion Reactive movement to a jet of fluid or gas.

K

keystone The central stone in the arch of a bridge or curved part of a building.

L

larva The immature stage in the life of many insects, amphibians, and fish.

lava Hot, molten rock emerging through volcanoes, known as magma when underground.

leading wheel The wheel at the front of a locomotive.

lens A transparent object, such as glass, that is curved on one or both sides. A lens bends and directs beams of light to form or alter the view of an image.

lever A long bar that moves around a pivot to help move a heavy object.

lift The force generated by an airfoil that counters the force of gravity and keeps a flying object in the air.

light spectrum The colors that light can be split into.

lithosphere The rigid outer shell of the Earth, including the crust and the rigid upper part of the mantle.

load The weight moved by a lever or other machine.

locomotive An engine powered by steam, diesel, or electricity, and used to pull the carriages of a train.

M

magma Hot, molten rock in the Earth's interior, known as lava when it emerges on the surface.

magnetism An invisible force found in some elements but especially in iron, which causes other pieces of iron to be either pushed apart or drawn together.

mantle The very deep layer of rock that lies underneath the Earth's crust.

mass The amount of matter there is in a substance or object. Mass is measured in pounds, tons, etc.

metamorphic rock Rock that has been chemically changed by heat and pressure to form a different rock.

metamorphosis Change, as in the life cycles of some animals, that involve a complete change of form, appearance, and other characteristics.

meteorologist A person who studies the science and patterns of weather and climate.

mineral A naturally occurring substance that is found in rocks.

mold A kind of fungus in the form of a woolly growth that is often found on stale and rotten food.

molten Something solid that has been melted, such as lava, which is molten rock.

monochrome Shades of black and white, with no other colors.

monorail A train that runs on a single rail.

mummy An embalmed or preserved body.

N

navigation The skill of plotting a route for a ship, aircraft, or other vehicle.

negative In photography, the image on the developed film from which photographic prints are made. The colors in a negative are reversed, so that dark areas appear to be light and light areas appear to be dark.

O

orbit In astronomy, the curved path followed by a planet or other body, around another planet or body.

order A major grouping of animals, larger than a family.

organism Any living thing, such as a plant or animal, that is capable of growth and reproducing itself.

osmosis The movement of a solvent, such as water, from a more dilute solution to a more concentrated one.

P

palaeontology The study of fossils.

photosynthesis The process by which plants make food using energy from sunlight.

piston A cylindrical device that moves up and down a cylinder, in response to the application and release of pressure from liquid or gas.

pivot A central point around which something revolves, balances, or sways.

plastic A durable, synthetic material that is easily molded and shaped by heat.

plumb line A string with a weight at one end that is used to check whether a building is vertical.

points Rails on the track that guide the wheels of a locomotive onto a different section of track.

precipitation Any form of water (rain, hail, sleet, and snow) that comes out of the air and falls to the ground.

primary colours Red, blue, and green, or magenta, cyan (blue), and yellow. These colors are the basis for all other shades and colors.

prism Specially shaped glass used to split white light into the spectrum, and to refract light rays away from their normal path.

propellant The fuel or force that causes something to go forward, such as the fuel in a rocket.

propeller A device, with blades, that rotate to provide thrust for a vehicle, such as a ship or plane.

prototype The first working model of a machine from a specific design.

pupa Inactive stage in the life cycle of many insects, such as butterflies and moths.

R

RAM (random access memory) Computer memory that holds data temporarily until the computer is switched off.

reflecting telescope A telescope that uses mirrors.

refracting telescope A telescope that uses lenses.

refraction The bending of light rays.

rolling stock The locomotives, carriages, wagons, and any other vehicles that operate on a railroad.

ROM (read-only memory) Computer memory that holds information permanently.

rudder A device for controlling the direction of a ship or plane.

S

satellite A celestial or artificial body that orbits around a planet or star.

savanna Tropical grassland.

sediment Solid particles of rock or other material.

sedimentary rock A rock that is made up of mineral particles that have been carried by wind and running water to accumulate in layers elsewhere, most commonly on the beds of lakes or in the seas and oceans.

seismology The study of earthquakes.

shutter Camera mechanism that controls the amount of time light is allowed to fall on the lens.

software Applications that allow computers to carry out specific tasks.

Solar system The family of planets, moons, and other bodies that orbit around the Sun.

solution A mixture of something solid and the liquid into which it has been completely dissolved.

sound wave Energy that transmits sound.

space probe A spacecraft that works in deep space.

space shuttle A vehicle designed to be used for at least 100 space flights.

space station A large, artificial satellite in which astronauts live and work.

species A group of animals that share similar characteristics and can breed successfully together.

steam traction Pulling movement achieved through the conversion of water to steam.

streamlined A shape that moves through air or water in the most efficient manner, with the least resistance from drag or friction.

T

tectonic plates The 20 or so giant slabs of rock that make up the Earth's surface.

tectonics The study of the structures that make up the Earth's surface.

thermometer An instrument for measuring temperature.

thorax The part of an insect's body between the head and the abdomen, which bears the wings and legs.

thrust The force that pushes something, such as an aircraft, forward.

tidal wave A huge ocean wave.

transpiration The process in the water cycle by which plants release water vapor into the air.

tropical A climate that is very hot and humid.

tropics Part of the Earth's surface that is between the Tropic of Cancer and the Tropic of Capricorn.

turbine A propeller like device that is driven by fast-moving gas currents, wind, and water.

turbulence Air or water movement that consists of eddies in random directions, with no smooth flow.

U

upthrust The force that makes a ship float or an aircraft take off.

V

valve A device that controls the flow of a liquid.

W

waterwheel A simple, water-driven turbine used to drive machinery.

weather The condition of the atmosphere at any particular time and place.

weathering The breakdown of rock and other materials when they are exposed to the weather.

weightlessness In space, a state in which an object has no actual weight, because it is not affected by gravitational attraction.

wind Air moving in relation to the Earth's surface.

windmill A machine for grinding and pumping, driven by vanes or sails that are moved by the wind.

Index

Acknowledgements

This edition is published by Southwater, an imprint of Anness Publishing Ltd,
Hermes House, 88–89 Blackfriars Road, London SE1 8HA;
tel. 020 7401 2077; fax 020 7633 9499
www.southwaterbooks.com; www.annesspublishing.com

If you like the images in this book and would like to investigate using
them for publishing, promotions or advertising, please visit our website
www.practicalpictures.com for more information.

UK agent: The Manning Partnership Ltd; tel. 01225 478444;
fax 01225 478440; sales@manning-partnership.co.uk
UK distributor: Grantham Book Services Ltd; tel. 01476 541080;
fax 01476 541061; orders@gbs.tbs-ltd.co.uk
North American agent/distributor: National Book Network;
tel. 301 459 3366; fax 301 429 5746; www.nbnbooks.com
Australian agent/distributor: Pan Macmillan Australia;
tel. 1300 135 113; fax 1300 135 103; customer.service@macmillan.com.au
New Zealand agent/distributor: David Bateman Ltd; tel. (09) 415 7664; fax (09) 415 8892

Publisher Joanna Lorenz
Managing Editor, Children's Books Gilly Cameron Cooper
Project Editor and Picture Researcher Rasha Elsaeed
Consultant Chris Oxlade
Contributing Authors Stephen Bennington, John Farndon, Ian Graham, Jen Green, Peter Harrison, Robin Kerrod,
Peter Mellett, Al Morrison, Chris Oxlade, Steve Parker, John Roston, Rodney Walshaw
Contributing Editors Gilly Cameron Cooper, Rebecca Clunes, Louisa Somerville, Joy Wotton
Editorial Readers Diane Ashmore, Jonathan Marshall, Richard McGinlay
Designer Sandra Marques/Axis Design Editions Ltd
Jacket Design Jonathan Davison
Photographers Paul Bricknell, John Freeman, Don Last, Tim Ridley
Nature Photographer Robert Pickett
Illustrators Cy Baker/Wildlife Art, Stephen Bennington, Peter Bull Art Studio, Stuart Carter,
Simon Gurr, Richard Hawke, Nick Hawken, Michael Lamb, Alan Male/Linden Artists, Guy Smith, Clive Spong, Stephen
Sweet/Simon Girling and Associates, Alisa Tingley, John Whetton
Stylists Ken Campbell, Jane Coney, Marion Elliot, Tim Grabham, Thomasina Smith,
Isolde Sommerfeldt, Melanie Williams

ETHICAL TRADING POLICY
Because of our ongoing ecological investment programme, you, as our customer, can have the pleasure and
reassurance of knowing that a tree is being cultivated on your behalf to naturally replace the materials used to make
the book you are holding. For further information about this scheme, go to www.annesspublishing.com/trees

A CIP catalogue record for this book is available from the British Library.

Previously published as *150 Great Science Experiments*

The publishers would like to thank all the children modelling in this book.

Picture Credits
b=bottom, t=top, c=centre, l=left, r=right
Bruce Coleman Ltd: 87cl. Frank Lane Picture Agency: 87bl, 96bl, 96bc, 96br. Nature Photographers Ltd: 76bc